GIORGIO'S MIRACLE

by Laurie Schmitt

D1602512

Illustrated by Kathryn Coyle

Available from:
Marian Helpers Center
Stockbridge, MA 01263

Prayerline: 1-800-804-3823
Orderline: 1-800-462-7426
Websites: TheDivineMercy.org
marian.org

ISBN: 978-1-59614-519-1
Marian Press Edition Publication date: May, 2020

Imprimi Potest:
Very Rev. Kazimierz Chwalek, MIC
Provincial Superior
The Blessed Virgin Mary, Mother of Mercy Province
September 10, 2019

Nihil Obstat:
Fr. Richard Drabik, MIC
Censor Deputatus
September 10, 2019

Dedication

For my husband and children,
all my love always

Acknowledgments

My special thanks to
- *my parents for handing on the Faith*
- *Judy, a true friend and soldier in Christ*
- *my children whose honest critique helped shape the story*
- *Angela for her encouragement when the manuscript was rough and unfinished*
- *my instructors at Catholic Distance University who made Church history come alive for me*

— Laurie Schmitt

Contents

1

Franca's Tricks

Giorgio wiggled his toes in the water. A chill went up his back, and he shivered, making him appreciate the woolen tunic that he wore. The moment he stepped into the creek, his feet felt like ice, but he marched further out into the little stream, scaring all of the minnows away. Water bugs were carried off with the ripples made by his footsteps. The brown mud of the creek bottom was squishy, and with every step it oozed up between his toes. By now, the bottom edges of his leggings were damp. The rounded pebbles under his feet were slimy with moss, giving him uneasy footing. Carefully, so as not to slip, he turned around to face his donkey and the two-wheeled cart, coaxing the animal to walk forward. "Come on, Franca! I know you don't like crossing the creek, but we've got to get this wagon to the inn!" Giorgio pleaded. "You're going to get us into trouble." With both hands, he tugged and tugged on the thin leather strap that was tied to Franca's halter.

Franca, the little brown donkey, was in a mischievous mood. She casually looked upstream, pretending to ignore Giorgio. Her eyes skimmed the lush scenery that surrounded her. In the meadow, just beyond the shoreline, alpine flowers nodded their heads to the cheerful breeze that caressed them. At this midmorning hour, the verdant pastures were dotted with sheep and goats, which were nonchalantly rambling among clumps of meadow grass, feeding as they meandered there. Well-ordered vineyards curled around the slopes and over small hills like smooth green ribbons. The fruit trees that grew in the orchards stood lined up in orderly rows, decorating the foothills for miles and leading Franca's eyes to take in the vista that beautified the far distance. The Apennine Mountain range stood majestic in the expanse to the west and beyond.

Franca bowed her head down to the fresh water and made funny slurping sounds as she took a long drink. Resisting his tugs for a minute more, she absentmindedly looked up at Giorgio. At last, she walked out into the stream, but when she got there, she halted midway and stood as if she were made of stone. She was positioned with all four of her legs in the water, while letting the cart stay on the rocky soil. Giorgio watched as the wheels of the cart settled into the gravelly shore under the bulk of its load. "Come on, hurry up. Don't you want to get home and be finished working for the morning?" Giorgio begged.

The little donkey turned her gaze upon Giorgio, but she held her place, obstinately refusing to move. To show her disapproval, she flexed her ears apart until they looked like a perfect letter V. Next, she sunk her feet as deep as she could into the muddy bottom of the stream. With her full weight, she leaned back toward the cart, making the rope between her and Giorgio become straight and tight. Her white muzzle barely quivered as she snuffled. "Are your feet cold yet?" she seemed to ask.

"You're up to your old tricks again, aren't you?" Giorgio said cheerfully. "So, it's tug-o-war, is it? Well, I'm not going to surrender! You're not going to win this game." Giorgio wrapped the leather straps around his hands a couple of times to secure his grip and steadied his footing by digging his freezing feet into the creek bottom. Puffs of dirty underwater clouds collected around his feet until the lazy current carried them away. "Come on, Franca! You think you're so smart, you silly donkey," Giorgio laughed at her entertaining contest.

Franca was clever, that was true, but in this game she had the special advantage of four sturdy legs, which gave her extra balance and stability. And if that was not enough, the heaviness of the cart acted like an anchor, ensuring that her stance was permanent. Franca held her place in the stream and pointed her ears at him and held them firm. Her tail, rhythmically swishing from side to side, was her only movement. She did not even blink. She was poised and waited good-naturedly for Giorgio's next move.

Franca could be so obstinate. Giorgio tugged on her lead rope, "Come on, Franca! Don't be so stubborn. We have stayed here long enough! Since when do you like getting your feet wet?" Giorgio was becoming frustrated. He did not want to be late with this delivery, and besides that, he was supposed to meet with Pietro as soon as he got back to the stable. Giorgio looked at Franca's skinny legs with her small, round hooves mired in the mud at the creek bottom. "You won't even budge one little inch! What am I going to do with you?" Giorgio asked. They stood quietly facing each other, neither one willing to adjust their positions.

Giorgio thought back to when he first attempted to train her to pull the cart. It was he, not his father, who was the champion on that day. His father, Alessandro, had traded some farm tools in exchange for Franca when she was still a young foal. He had hoped that she would one day be capable of pulling the cart and making deliveries for his blacksmith shop and the inn, but Franca was afraid of big Alessandro. He had no luck in getting her to wear the harness. She shied away from him whenever he came near to her. In those days, Franca would stand in the stable, resolute and stiff legged — just as she was doing now. Alessandro worked and worked with Franca until he became tired and disinterested. His patience was all but used up, and he was ready to give up on Franca altogether, but Giorgio begged if he could have a chance with her. Alessandro consented and let Giorgio try his luck.

Giorgio took his father's place next to Franca and calmly petted her neck and rubbed her muzzle, talking affectionately to her the whole time. He brushed her back and softly patted her legs. After building up her trust, he was able to get her to relax and step forward by giving her a small piece of an apple. That's all it took. He easily slipped the harness over her and hitched her to the little cart. Alessandro was amazed at the swiftness of Giorgio's work. Alessandro opened the stable doors and out walked Giorgio, with Franca pulling the wagon behind her. From then on, Giorgio and Franca were best of friends. Even though Alessandro owned Franca, she belonged heart and soul to Giorgio.

Giorgio thought about how Franca loved eating from his hand, especially if he had something sweet. "That's it! Why didn't I think of it before?" he said out loud. "Hold on now, Franca." He braced himself. With one hand stretching the lead rope taut, he reached behind himself and grabbed his leather satchel that was slung over his shoulders. He kept his eyes locked on Franca as he fumbled blindly in the pouch. She blinked at him as if she was saying, "Finally, you funny boy! What took you so long?"

Giorgio's fingers got hold of a small carrot and he held it out to Franca. She caught sight of it, and without any warning at all, Franca lurched forward. It all happened so suddenly that Giorgio was taken by surprise. He still was keeping a firm grip on the rope, and when it slackened, his feet gave way. He slipped and lost his balance, falling sideways into the knee-high water and making a huge splash. Giorgio was drenched from head to toe. He came sputtering out of the creek, jumping up as fast as he was able. The icy water poured off of him. His satchel was so full of the liquid that it looked ready to burst. "Franca!" he gasped, sputtering drops of water in every direction, "Very funny! You and your jokes. What did I ever do to you?"

Franca had triumphantly snatched the orange carrot from Giorgio before he fell, and she quickly gobbled it down. Nothing remained of it except the leaves that hung out of one side of Franca's mouth. She impishly mocked him by fixing her ears and making them look like one straight horizontal line across the top of her head. Next, she twisted her jaw creating a comic grin and presenting her yellowed and oversized teeth. She brayed her "Ee Aw! Ee Aw!" as if to say, "I win again!"

Giorgio stood up. The brim of his leather hat, now fully saturated and trickling out water, drooped down over his ears. His curly black hair was sopping wet and flattened to his head, covering his eyes like a mask. Water dribbled out from his sleeves and the bottom of the tunic. Giorgio's drenched clothing stuck to his skin and was making him feel itchy. As he stood there with water running down his chin, he had to smile. "Franca!" Giorgio said as he pushed the hair from his eyes. "No fair! Some best friend you are."

Franca wagged her head from side to side as she hiked through the creek, towing the cart of vegetables and fruit behind her. As she passed Giorgio, she snickered. To Giorgio, it sounded like she was chuckling to herself, "Ha, ha, ha!" Giorgio dumped the water from his satchel and pulled off his hat to wring it out, realizing that someone else was laughing, too.

"Hey, Giorgio! Great day to take a bath! Ha!" Pietro yelled. There was Pietro, standing on the lane that led to town, hunched over and holding his ribs because he was giggling so hard. His red cap had fallen off, and as he picked it up, he slapped it against his leg to dust it off and plunked it back on his head. "That," Pietro said in laughter, "was the funniest thing I've seen in a long time!"

"Well, so glad you appreciated it." Giorgio, acting as seriously as he could, said, "It's not too often a fella gets to take a bath and wash his clothes at the same time." Giorgio's feet stumbled against the slippery rocks as he clumsily made his way out of the creek. He took his place next to Franca, now quite glad for the warm morning sun. "You came this far out of town just to see this, I suppose?" Giorgio asked. With water still dripping down his face and out of his clothing, he could not help but smile at what had just happened.

"No," Pietro laughed, "I came racing all the way because I couldn't wait to tell you that my father has given me permission to study with you, so long as I keep up with my chores. And he is letting me use his brother's old Latin primer. If I can learn my Latin, then for sure I can be a priest someday, just like my uncle!"

"That's perfect! I can teach you the little I know, but maybe Don Bartolomeo will help us both. Maybe he has a prayer book that he'd let us borrow. I'm planning on visiting him this afternoon and will talk with him about it."

"Thanks, Giorgio." Pietro adjusted the single leather strap attached to his breeches. It ran across his back and liked to slip off his shoulder

sometimes. As the two boys walked together
with Franca in between them, little dust clouds
rose from under their bare feet.

Giorgio looked up at the sun in the sky,
saying, "We better hurry on our way. We've
got to get this cartload to the inn before the
noon *Angelus* bells ring." Franca was still feeling victorious, and when Giorgio tapped her
rump, she easily broke into a trot, making both
Giorgio and Pietro jog along beside her. The
boys did not talk now. Both were happy and
thinking of the afternoon ahead.

2

Life in Turin

As they passed through the gates of Turin, the two boys parted ways. Pietro was off to do his chores at home, and later on he would be in the public square, helping his father by tending his shop. After unloading the cart at the inn, Giorgio would be expected to check on the horses in the stable. Then he and Franca could rest from their duties for a while. Franca sensed that their morning's work was almost done and picked up her pace.

Giorgio and Franca worked together every day but still made time for fun. When Franca was a young foal, Giorgio trained her to perform some special acts. It all started when she would get tired of waiting for something to eat. She would paw the ground in front of her for three beats. Giorgio got the idea that if he rewarded her, she would be likely to tap the ground when-ever he asked her to. After they had practiced the routine often, Giorgio would ask Franca to count to three in front of interested listeners. The little children of Turin thought Franca was so brilliant when she obeyed him. "She's so good at counting," the little children marveled. "What a smart little donkey!"

Giorgio would ask her math problems that equaled three. He would say things like, "Franca, what is one plus two?" or "Franca, what is seven take away four?"

But Franca had her limitations, and Giorgio knew when her attitude toward the game was changing. She would only perform the count-to-three act for so long. Then, she would not pound the ground three times but would stamp only once, as if to say, "This game is now over."

Giorgio learned how to read Franca's mood and so mastered the timing of the game. When he sensed that she was tired of playing, first he would say to her, "Franca, what is two plus two?" For the last time, the animal would pound out three definite beats. Next Giorgio would say, "Now Franca, that answer is not correct. Come on, you know what it is."

Then, Franca would promptly tap one more beat to show her frustration. "Enough of this game. Give me something sweet now!" she seemed to say.

Giorgio would act proud of Franca, as if she had solved the math problem. He would say, "That's right, Franca! The answer is four. What a clever donkey you are!"

The little children would hug her neck and brush their hands over her strong back. They were so impressed at her talent. They all loved Franca. The merchants of the village square also enjoyed the pranks of Giorgio and Franca. "Here is Giorgio and his intelligent little donkey," they would say whenever they would see the two coming their way. The older people were glad to see the loving bond between a boy and his pet. It made them feel happy for a little while, but it was another trick Franca performed that made the people pause for a moment from the problems of their day. Their wonderment had to do with the ringing of the church bells.

In Turin, the bells of St. Silvestro's church would toll at the hours of the *Angelus* prayer. The bells would first toll at six o'clock in the morning, then again at noon, and lastly at six o'clock in the evening. Three times each day, the bells would chime specially to remind the people to pray and thank God for His many gifts. Giorgio had trained Franca to bow down and kneel at the tolling of the six o'clock evening bell. As the townspeople observed the animal bending low, they felt conviction in their hearts. "What do I believe? Where is my faith?" they wondered to themselves. Although Franca seemed reverent when bowing to the sound of the bells, the truth was that Franca was motivated only by her stomach. Giorgio was able to get her to perform this act because he rewarded her immediately with lumps of sugar. It seemed to Giorgio that Franca would do almost anything for a treat.

Giorgio turned sharply away from his ponderings and down the narrow alley which led to the back door of the inn. Franca's cart scraped against the stone wall, but Giorgio did not seem to notice. "I like it best when we go to the outskirts of Turin," Giorgio said to Franca, "visiting with the farmers and bringing back apples, olives, grapes and all sorts of vegetables that Aunt Gemma needs for her kitchen. But I suppose that's your favorite too, because it means treats for you, right, Franca?" He paused for a moment and petted her, as if he was giving Franca a chance to respond. She bent her ears forward, but did not make a sound.

"Here we are," Giorgio said as they approached the back door of the inn, the Bella Vista. "Hold still so I can unload the cart." Franca rested as he emptied the cart. It bounced and wobbled a little as Giorgio worked. Her muscles twitched now and then to ward off flies and gnats, but otherwise, she stood still, with her head down. She was ready for a rest.

Giorgio hauled the produce and other goods into the storeroom of Gemma's kitchen. Aunt Gemma met Giorgio at the door, reached out for him, and rumpled his hair. "When you are done hauling everything in, come and have something to eat with me. We have time before the guests sit down," she said.

Giorgio went back to the cart and lifted a sack of freshly ground wheat. He carried it over the threshold and set it down in the storeroom. He looked into the kitchen.

It was dimly lit by the tallow candles mounted on the walls. The hearth fire was glowing and above it, a small cauldron of the day's stew simmered. Its spicy aroma filled the air. The huge table was nicely laid out for the guests of the inn, who would soon be coming.

Gemma set a bowl of stew at the table for Giorgio. They prayed together and began eating.

"We have new guests at the inn this morning," Gemma said. "Your father wants to make sure you tend to their horses. He is already at the blacksmith shop repairing their wagon."

"I'll be sure to check on the horses when Franca and I return to the stable," Giorgio said. His thoughts turned toward his father, Alessandro. He worked long, hard days in the heat and smoke of his fire. He was a muscular man, rough and rugged. As he pounded searing hot pieces of iron against the heavy anvil, sparks would fly. He worked every day making tools and repairing all sorts of useful things. He was excellent at his craft and well -respected by the villagers, yet he seemed angry at the world, angry at almighty God Himself. Gemma looked across the table at Giorgio. She had taken care of him since his mother had died, so she knew him well. She could sense that something was troubling him. "What are you thinking about?" she asked.

Giorgio turned to her and spoke what was on his mind. "Aunt Gemma, I never feel good about the work I do for my father. I don't think I'll ever do anything right for him. No matter how I try, I cannot please him."

Gemma tried to cheer Giorgio up. "Giorgio, don't be hard on yourself; it's not anything you've done. Your father sometimes takes his work too seriously. He is tired and overworked."

Gemma also understood her brother, Alessandro, and silently vowed that she must talk with him. She considered what might be bothering him. When Giorgio's mother had died, it seemed that Alessandro lost all interest in everything. He quit attending Mass and instead poured himself into his work. Gemma resolved to be strict with her older brother, to tell him what he needed to hear.

She could see Giorgio's concern for his father and empathized with him. She wanted him to feel better and tried to cheer him up. "Don't be troubled," she said. "Your father was happy once, and he will be again one day." She smiled and looked around the kitchen. "I remember when we were young. We played together here in this very inn. Our parents owned both the Bella Vista and the blacksmith shop in those days. They loved us, and together we worked. Those were happy days for all of us."

Giorgio smiled at her and got up from the table. "Thank you, Aunt Gemma," Giorgio said. "It's time for me to go to the stable. Franca's thirsty and tired."

He hugged Gemma and left the kitchen, going out to meet Franca, who was waiting patiently for him. Franca brayed a happy "Ee Aw!" as she saw him coming. She tossed her head up and down. Giorgio patted her neck and grabbed the lead rope. As the cart wheeled around to head back to the square, Giorgio said, "Aren't you glad you have me for your friend? Things could be worse for you. Just think if you were a farmer's donkey. You'd have to work even harder than you do now ... all day in the hot sun. You should thank me."

Franca nuzzled Giorgio. "Thank you," she seemed to say.

Giorgio hugged her neck and said, "And you're welcome."

The two of them headed to the stable and the blacksmith shop. These were located on the edge of the *Piazza di Grano* and stood facing the old church. Saint Silvestro's was a beautiful church. Its sun-bleached facade cheerily invited the people to enter. The bells from their tower chimed for the *Angelus* three times each day, and again before Mass would begin. It seemed like the merchants and vendors set their hours by the predictable sound of the church bells.

As Giorgio led Franca through the square, the *Angelus* bells rang for the noon prayer. Giorgio said, "Well, Franca, we're right on time." The bells always brought Giorgio a silent joy. He paused, bowed his head, and prayed, "*Angelus Domini nuntiavit Mariae. Et concepit de Spiritu Sancto. Ave Maria, gratia plena; Dominus tecum ...* "

After finishing the prayer, Giorgio looked at the beautiful old church across the square.

"Here, someday soon, I hope that my father will feel happiness again ... even though today, the church and its bells seem not to have any effect on him."

Giorgio's father was like the other towns-people of Turin, losing faith in God, no longer appreciating the simple things of life. They grumbled if the weather was too dry or when it was too wet. The average man of Turin was sad at heart. Giorgio looked up into the heavens above him and wondered out loud, "How is it that people's hearts could be shut to God's miracles? It would take a true miracle, Franca, to change the hardened hearts of the people of Turin. So, that is what I am praying for: a true miracle."

Giorgio and Franca arrived at the stable, looking forward to an afternoon rest. Franca was ready to be free of the cart. "Well, Franca," Giorgio said, "let's go into the stable and get this cart off. There'll be no more work for you today, so you can take a well-deserved break."

As soon as they were in the stable, Giorgio unhitched the wagon and harness. He led Franca into her stall and took off her halter. She took a long drink of water and then set about munching some hay. Giorgio went to the other horses in the stable and made sure each had clean water and fodder in its manger. He spoke calmingly to each one as he brushed its mane and neck. After his work was done, he settled himself comfortably in a pile of fresh straw. The air was still. Giorgio watched the specks of dust dance in the hazy shafts of light that glinted through the cracks of the stable door. The hot June day made him glad to be out of the sun's heat. Giorgio thought about his father and his gruff way and remembered what Gemma had told Giorgio. He leaned back into the straw and shut his eyes, trying to imagine his father as a young boy, probably doing the same chores as Giorgio. Not much had changed at the inn since his grandparents had owned it. Even this stable was a place where his grandfather would have worked. The same old beams held up the roof, and the same wooden boards made the stalls. He wondered if his own father had rested in straw as he was doing now. Giorgio closed his eyes tightly and tried to imagine his mother's face. Yet as hard as he tried, he could not. He had never met his mother, but he loved her. Deep in his heart, he knew she was watching out for him and waiting for him. He believed he would see her someday in Heaven, and what a happy day that would be!

He and Franca had rested long enough. Giorgio got up and brushed off the bits of straw that clung to his clothes. He smoothed his hand over Franca's ears to remove the dusty chaff. Her long, silky ears felt velvety to the touch. Giorgio slipped the halter over her head and tied on the lead rope. He led her out the stable door, saying, "No cart for this trip. Come on. We'll go and talk with Don Bartolomeo."

Franca gladly followed him out. Together, the two of them headed across the square to St. Silvestro's church.

3

Crossing the Square

The *Piazza di Grano* was one of the busiest places in Turin, and crossing it was not easy because dense crowds of people gathered there daily. Today, the sky above the *piazza* displayed itself dressed in baby blue and filled with fluffy, cumulous clouds that tumbled with the wind's breath, promising fair weather. The ancient cobblestone that made up the courtyard floor contrasted rudely with the softness of the vault overhead. Bricks that covered the ground in the square had settled over the years and had become uneven in places. The extensive quad was walled in by the steady row of old stone buildings that permanently fixed its edges.

Giorgio inhaled the sweet odor of fresh-cut flowers as he walked by a little shop. Looking up, he regarded the pretty bouquets of multi-colored flowers that added a flourish of color to the scene. Floral garlands and assorted blossoms were thriving in the window boxes that hung high above the ground from every balcony of the two- and three-story buildings.

Throughout the square, stonework pillars and tall cylindrical colonnades reinforced the heaviest, highest structures, while at the same time providing for the passers by a shady walkway within the beautiful porticos. In the distance ahead of him, Giorgio spied one of these shady spaces that offered a comfortable place for spectators to dine *al fresco*. A few noblemen and their elegant ladies sat, enjoying glasses of red wine. At another table, a small group of travelers feasted together. From where he walked, Giorgio could hear them marveling at the old fountain that stood prominently in the exact center of the square. The fountain boasted a marble sculpture of a Roman soldier astride his warhorse, his lance raised and equipped for victory. The fountain was a popular spot for people to meet each other.

The square was a place of both exceptional beauty and commonplace efficiency. Here was the center of local business trade, for in this section of Turin, the townspeople would barter for goods and haggle with each other until each party was satisfied. The trade deal was complete when together both parties agreed as to the value of whatever it was they were exchanging. Merchants of Turin swapped their handmade goods with the local farmers and shepherds in exchange for grains and livestock, and in turn, the people from the countryside took home with them tools and other supplies they needed for their livelihood.

Giorgio and Franca continued through the square listening to folks chatter. Here, people came to catch up on the latest news. Friends met with friends, telling each other their troubles and sharing any good news they might have. Boys and girls would come with their parents to help out. When their parents had no work for them to do, the children would congregate and play games. Sometimes, they would have races with each other on the outer edges of the square.

As Giorgio and Franca made their way across, Giorgio stopped at the tack and saddlery shop and looked at the leather goods hanging on the wall. Franca's strap that hooked to her halter was wearing thin, and he knew it would have to be replaced someday soon. "Good day, Giorgio," the grumpy shop owner said. The man had a mind for business and quickly pointed to his cache of goods. He held some things out to Giorgio, eager to make a sale. "Did something catch your eye? Maybe a new harness, or a halter, perhaps, for the donkey?"

The man was unpleasant and forced his wares on Giorgio. Like the average person in

Turin, he cared only for the day at hand and had
little concern for anything other than his livelihood. This man was dismal, and listening to
him talk about how bleak and futile his life was
would only depress Giorgio. He turned back to
the square, saying, "No, thank you, not today.
We're just passing by."

As he looked over the man's shoulder, Giorgio noticed three children playing catch with a
little ball. Pietro was among them. He was easy
to see, for he always wore his red cap. The boys
were so focused on their game that not one of
the three boys noticed the shaggy little brown
and white dog watching them. The dog's eyes
were firmly set on the ball, and each time it
bounced up from the cobblestone, his head
followed its movement. His tongue hung out
of one side of his mouth as he watched. Play-
ful excitement welled up in the pup. His bushy
tail wagged back and forth, sweeping across the
cobblestones as he sat impatiently, following
the ball's every move. Finally, he stood up on
his hind legs and whimpered as if he was asking
to be invited to play. The dog's interest in the
game grew until he could not keep himself from
joining in. In a split second, the dog lunged for
the ball, caught it up in his mouth, and ran just

out of reach of Pietro. He crouched wagging and begging for attention.

Both the shopkeeper and Giorgio watched the frisky dog and were curious to see what would happen next. The shopkeeper was annoyed. Under his breath, he said, "Hmm ... looks like a match of three against one."

Giorgio stepped away from the man and out into the plaza, remembering Franca's trick on him earlier that day, and he smiled as he called out. "Hey, Pietro, looks like he wants to play, too. Do you think you can catch him? I bet he's faster than you!" Giorgio's taunts broke their concentration and made the three young boys ready for the challenge.

"Come here, pup, come here. Give us back the ball," the tallest boy coaxed.

The dog, with the ball in its mouth, gave a muffled bark. "You can't catch me!" he seemed to say.

The second boy took small and steady steps, trying to sneak closer to the dog in hopes of grabbing the ball. "Come here ... come on fella'," he said. But the furry dog dodged out of the way just before the boy was within arm's reach.

Pietro adjusted his hat and said, "Come on, boys! Let's get him!"

With that, the dog crouched low and made a couple of small grunting sounds, as if to say, "The chase is on. Come on. I dare you to get this ball." Suddenly, the canine jumped up in midair and bolted away. He ran well out of range of the boys and stopped short, turning around to make sure the boys were after him. The energetic dog was enjoying himself.

The boys took the animal's proposition seriously. They raced after it through the town square, determined to get the ball back. Several makeshift tents were set in the busy plaza. The dog ran under a table set with tin-ware and pottery. The metal things rattled as he scampered under the table, and a few clay pots fell off and crashed on the ground. An old woman hollered after the boys, "Come back here, you ragamuffins! I'll tell your fathers what you've done!" She grabbed her broom and lifted it high in the air as she yelled. She ran after them for a few short steps and then started sweeping up the broken pottery. Giorgio stopped to help her. He gathered up the shards and set them in a mound. Giorgio reached for the broom, but she insisted on doing her own work. "Times are hard enough! I can't afford my goods to be ruined," she said. She lifted her head and saw that the chase continued. "It's one bad thing after another. What's the use in trying anymore?" she wondered out loud.

After the crash of the pottery, all of the vendors were on guard and watched the chase with personal interest. The man selling woolen rugs cried, "Stop! Get away! Out of the square with you!"

Giorgio and Franca kept to the outer border of the courtyard. The little dog rushed happily by them and ran through several small shops.

Some sold jewelry and stringed instruments, while others offered things made of wood. The man in charge of the saddlery and tack shop, who just moments earlier had forced himself to be courteous to Giorgio, now grabbed a whip and made its sound splinter the air. It hissed and cracked, causing everyone to turn their heads. The dread of the old man's wrath only made the furry dog and the three boys move faster. Franca jolted and turned at the snap of the whip. Giorgio walked her away from the scene and toward the church.

The harder the boys raced and dashed about, the happier and livelier the little dog became. The merchants realized this game of chase was not going to stop any time soon. People were shouting and scurrying around. As he passed by the merchants, Giorgio did whatever he could to help them. He picked up a few woolen rugs that had fallen from their stack. He steadied an unstable display which showed beautiful oil portraits. Some of the vendors grabbed hold of the goods that they exhibited while others waved brooms and farming tools at the small, wild troupe. The distressed crowd grumbled about the broken things, as if that was all that mattered to them. Neither the dog nor the boys slowed down.

They tore past the booth where Pietro's father had some of his goods hanging. He was a tailor and sold garments and locally woven cloth. Some beautiful silks and satins from traders in Genoa were there. Pietro's father pleaded, "Enough! Pietro! Stop!" As the dog ran through the fabrics, a blue silk scarf became draped around his neck. It was trailing and flapping behind him like a flag as he ran on and on. Pietro was pulled out of the game by his father. "No more gallivanting for you!"

Pietro stood by his father and watched the two boys do their best to catch the dog. Every few steps he stopped and turned to see if they were getting closer to him, and then he would dive off again in a flash. The dog would not allow the two boys to get an inch nearer. By now, the angered merchants joined in the chase. They formed a riotous mob and made an attempt to corner the animal, but he escaped by jumping over a table of bakery goods. The entire crowd was shouting, "Stop! Catch that dog!"

Some of the merchants safeguarded their goods by lying on top of their tables. Giorgio helped the peasants throw blankets over their assorted handiwork in hopes of keeping it safe. The vendors selling fresh meat stood now in front

of their stalls, shooing the reckless crew away.
"Get away from here! Away!" they boomed,
waving their aprons at the wild runners.

There was a long table filled with special
fruit that was hauled in from Genoa. Things like
oranges and lemons grew on the warm southern
coast near the sea. One of the boys knocked over
a basket of brightly colored apricots. They rolled
everywhere across the courtyard. Franca happily
stretched down, picked one up, and ate it as she
watched the chase go on. Finally, the little dog
realized he was outnumbered and disappeared
down a side street, still carrying the ball. The
chase came to an end. Giorgio saw Pietro pick
up the dirty blue scarf to bring it back to his
father's stand. No doubt Pietro and the other
boys would have to help the vendors get the
square in order again.

Pietro stood in front of his father. He realized how quickly the game had gotten out of
hand and silently vowed he would never again
let himself become part of such antics. He was
ashamed of his behavior, and his father could tell
just by looking at him. "Pietro," his father said
quietly, "how is it that you will be a priest someday? With this kind of performance? Who will
rely on you if you let yourself get carried away

with this sort of caper?" He could see that Pietro understood the gravity of his actions, and so the man finished, saying, "Go and help the others to get their things picked up and sorted. We will talk more of this when the day is done."

Giorgio had enough of the wild game, and he and Franca made their way through the frantic crowd. He felt responsible for encouraging it. "The chase started out looking like fun. I shouldn't have put the boys up to it. I feel sorry for Pietro," he said to Franca. "Our time with him may likely be put off for a while." Giorgio turned around and took one last look at the fiasco. The courtyard was a mess, but crews of people were teaming to clean it up.

Giorgio and Franca slowly walked past the cobbler's shop, the last place on the corner of the square. When they came to the front of St. Silvestro's, Giorgio took in the majesty of its height. The church offered security and rest to Giorgio and to anyone else who would enter in. Some people were shuffling into the old church. He looked over his shoulder and saw a few people coming from the square to make a visit. Others came from the narrow streets surrounding the square. They all entered through the front doors, but Giorgio wanted to tie Franca behind the church, so they walked on toward the side entry. He hoped he might meet Don Bartolomeo there. Giorgio was anxious to talk with him.

4

Don Bartolomeo

Giorgio and Franca turned at the church's corner and walked down the narrow passage that ran alongside of it, leading to the area where Franca could be tied. Here, Giorgio could see the rectory, which stood on the other side of the small, grassy plot. Little indigo and cream-colored flowers were blossoming around an alcove enshrining a figure of the Blessed Mother. The scent of the flowers added an enchanting fragrance to the air. It was peaceful here and quiet, except for the

bubbling sound of the stone fountain and a few
doves cooing from the nearby rooftops. Giorgio
led Franca to a tall tree and tied her lead rope to
it. He was not sure if Don Bartolomeo was in
the rectory or in the church, so Giorgio opted
to make a visit to the church first. He thought
of his talk with Gemma in her kitchen and wondered again about his father. The day's events
brought him into a somber mood. He was in
need of some wordless prayer, and the church
would offer a welcome break from the bright
afternoon sunshine. And then, he was sure, Don
Bartolomeo would be able to answer the questions that troubled him.

"Here's some grass for you to feed on while
I'm gone, but don't eat the flowers. A nice
breeze is blowing and that will help cool you,
Franca. I won't be long." The shadow of the
church covered the tall tree. With that, Giorgio
brushed his hand over Franca's neck and turned
toward the church. He leaped up the steps and
grasped for the side door, taking one last look
at Franca. She had made herself comfortable
by lying down on the grass. Even now her eyes
were closed.

Giorgio pushed through the heavy wooden
doors of the church, feeling like he was entering

another realm. He tried to be silent, but the old doors creaked as he made his way in. It took a few seconds for his eyes to adjust to the dimness. The interior of the church was in sharp contrast to the world outside. The air was much cooler and filled with the sweet-smelling odor of incense. It beckoned him to enter in. The tall arches and high cupolas pulled his thoughts heavenward. He sat in amazement as he gazed around at the beauty that engulfed him, as if this was his first visit to this church. Here, it was all stillness and peace. A few candles were lit on the high altar, giving off a faint warm glow. The sacristy lamp gleamed softly. Now and then people slipped into the church and settled quietly for prayer before the Blessed Sacrament.

Giorgio often visited the church alone. The aged wood of the pews was well worn and smooth. As he knelt, he wondered how many other people had come here since the church had been built, just like he did, to retreat from the world outside. Here, he was certain that his prayers for his mother and Gemma, for Franca and his other friends, and his father, too, were heard and answered. He looked at the high altar and its intricate carvings. He was amazed at the beauty of the angelic sculptures. Saint Michael was probably his favorite, he thought. The side altars for the Blessed Virgin and of St. Joseph were decorated with marble altars and gold trimmings. Both altars had bouquets of freshly cut flowers, serving as a reminder of how God loves his creation.

Giorgio knelt in the pew and bowed his head in prayer. He felt his mind and body slow down. He looked up at the crucifix hanging above the altar just in time to see Don Bartolomeo walking noiselessly from the sacristy and carrying a large book. He quietly placed it on one of the side altars and then disappeared again into the sacristy. Giorgio prayed the priest would have time to talk with him.

Don Bartolomeo was one of Giorgio's best friends. He was a young Italian priest who was happy to be ministering to the people of Turin. He loved his vocation and worked tirelessly to encourage the people to come back to the Mass. Often throughout the day, the priest would go into the market square wearing his black cassock with his *cappello Romano* atop his head and converse with the merchants and peasants that happened to be there. They knew him to be sincere. He wanted to know what was on their minds, how their families were, and of any concerns they may have. Together, Don Bartolomeo and the people would talk about how local business was faring or how the crops were doing and discuss the most recent happenings in Turin and the area around it. The priest was well respected by all the townspeople, and yet so many could not bring themselves back to the faith. He tried to understand the people. Life was hard for so many. He, like Giorgio, prayed for a miracle.

Giorgio crossed himself and slipped into the sacristy. Don Bartolomeo grinned and greeted Giorgio, giving him a firm but friendly pat on the back. "How's my Giorgio today! And where's Franca? I wonder that someday your little donkey will come into the church with you!" Don Bartolomeo said in jest.

"Oh, she is tied up behind the church, waiting for me." Giorgio smiled at the picture in his mind of Franca standing in the church.

Don Bartolomeo continued putting books and other religious articles in their proper places. He asked, "What can I do for you today? Is this visit one of business or pleasure?"

"Well, it's a little bit of both, I suppose. For one thing, Pietro and I are hoping you could spare one of your prayer books. You know Pietro always talks about the priesthood, so we thought we could study together. We would like to know our Latin prayers well."

"Yes, I do have one in the rectory that you could borrow, and I'll make a point to talk with Pietro's father. Perhaps you both would do well with private tutoring. I was just going in to have something to eat. Do you have time to have a little supper with me?" the priest asked.

"Yes, that would be nice. That means you have time to talk with me," Giorgio said.

"Oh, yes," the priest joked. "Time to talk and to listen. No doubt you have some good stories to tell." Don Bartolomeo's eyes sparkled as he joked with Giorgio.

Giorgio always shared his latest adventures with Don Bartolomeo. He felt he was able to talk to the priest about anything. Together, they exited through the side door and walked to the rectory. They both took note of Franca, who by now was standing under the tree, flicking her oversized ears to keep buzzing pests away. Giorgio followed the priest in and settled at the old, wooden table in the kitchen. Don Bartolomeo set out some bread and cheese.

"The bread you will know as it was made fresh today by your Aunt Gemma's hands,"

Don Bartolomeo explained, "but the soup I have made myself."

With that, Don Bartolomeo set out two wooden bowls and ladled in the vegetable soup. After saying grace together, Don Bartolomeo looked again at Giorgio. "You have a thoughtful look about you today. Something is on your mind. What is it?" he asked.

Giorgio looked into the kind eyes of the priest. "I am curious about something. I've been thinking about it for a long while. Did you know my mother well? Can you tell me about her?" he asked.

"Of course, I knew her, but not well, for I was new to St. Silvestro's in those days. The first time I met her was when she and your father came to arrange for your Baptism. They were both so happy, anticipating that day." The priest paused for a moment and, softening his tone of voice, continued, "Sadly, she died when you were only a few days old." He kept silent, letting his words have their effect on Giorgio. "Over time I have gotten to know your father and Aunt Gemma. He saw to it that you were baptized here, but I think it was more for the sake of your mother's memory than anything else. He grieved her loss all that winter, and now he can scarcely bring

himself to walk on the same side of the street
that the church stands on. What makes you ask
something so weighty, Giorgio?"

"Sometimes I wonder about her, that's all
… and my father. It's just that he seems cross
all the time. Aunt Gemma tells me he used to
be easy to be with, but now it seems all I do is
disappoint him. There is hardly anything that I
can do to please him."

"Oftentimes people can blame others for
the difficulties in their own lives. They fail to
see God's love is bigger than just this world."
The priest could see that Giorgio was deep in
thought. He followed Giorgio's eyes as they
wandered about the room, taking in the few
furnishings. The kitchen where they sat boasted
only a small work table and two chairs. Giorgio
looked through the doorway into the parlor. He
could see the beautiful artwork that adorned
the walls. Religious themed paintings of the
Transfiguration and the Flight into Egypt were
expertly done.

After a moment, Giorgio sat forward in his
chair and looked into the priest's eyes. "Don
Bartolomeo, how can it be that the people of
Turin seem so far away from God? Sometimes
I wonder if there is anyone — besides Aunt

Gemma and you — who is always happy, always at peace."

Don Bartolomeo set down his piece of bread, rested his arms on the table, and folded his hands. "Well, Giorgio," he said, "we mustn't be too hard on them. Sometimes people forget. They forget to take their problems, the sorrows of their hearts, to God in prayer. But there is also very real danger." The priest paused for a moment, carefully considering what he would say next. "Do you know of the latest news? News that the Turks have captured Constantinople just last week? The city fell on May 29, the Feast of Pentecost. Many people have died. The town is in ruins. Holy sites have been forever destroyed."

"No, I hadn't heard. That's terrible news ... what will happen now?" Giorgio asked.

"This is part of what is laying on the hearts of the people. From the ambo of St. John the Baptist Cathedral, our Bishop Ludovico has preached to those who would hear. Pope Nicholas V has tried to unite all of Christendom in defense of that city, but it seems that the people are absorbed in their own business trade and their own problems," the priest said sadly. "Here it is one city-state, one village, against another."

Giorgio pushed himself away from the table. He tried to understand.

"You see, Giorgio," Don Bartolomeo persisted, "the people are burdened. They are fearful. There are dreadful losses to other villages near to ours that unsettle the minds of the people here in Turin. Whole villages are destroyed. Hardworking people are forced to flee, leaving behind them the only life they have known. Many innocent people are suffering. In these times, it seems to them that the wars are the only thing that we can depend upon. People have lost hope. The feeling of injustice hangs in the air."

The young priest was always wise and kind in his responses, Giorgio thought, for he knew that Don Bartolomeo prayed day and night for the people of Turin. It was his heart's desire that they would come back to the fullness of the faith. For this, he worked tirelessly.

"Why do they keep themselves from God?" Giorgio wondered aloud. "I am glad the *Angelus* bells ring. It is like God is softly calling each of us to Him."

The talk between Giorgio and Don Bartolomeo continued well into the evening. Both had lost track of time, so it was in a rush that

Giorgio left the rectory with the treasured book and went to where he had tied Franca a few hours earlier.

5

Franca's Journey

While Giorgio and Don Bartolomeo were talking together, Franca was losing her patience with being tied up for so long. She was now well-rested, tired of getting bug-bitten, and desperately wanting to exercise her legs. She decided that she had stood under the tall tree for long enough and so pulled against the leather strap that held her bound. She pawed the ground, turning up tufts of grass.

The vendors in the *piazza* were packing up for the day. One by one, Franca could hear their old wooden carts creaking as they passed by the narrow opening, through which she could see the square. The wagon wheels whirred and clunked as they were pulled across the well-traveled route. The area was smooth for only a step or two. Rough patches appeared where the stones had settled and shifted over time. She could smell the fruit and vegetables and made up her mind to find something to eat. Franca stepped backwards and yanked hard. She worked for a few minutes, pulling against the tree, straining until the worn leather band that was tied to her halter tore apart. It fell on the ground in a hush, and, as if to make up for its silent landing, she sounded off, braying her raspy "Ee Aw! Ee Aw!" and shaking her head from side to side. Her coarse mane flopped back and forth and then stood in a stiff, frizzy line down her neck. Now that she was finally free, she wandered. She walked down the narrow pass between the buildings and came into the *piazza*. She beelined to the fountain in the square and took a long drink of the cool water.

A merchant was passing by and hollered, "Hey there! Out of the fountain! Get along now!" Franca bolted and kicked her back legs high into the air. Her hooves made clipping sounds as she sauntered across the cobblestone.

Three village children from the market square were heading home for their supper and evening chores, and they took notice of Franca. They huddled around her. The youngest boy, one of the three who had been chasing the spirited dog earlier that day, patted Franca on her neck. He pulled her long, bristly mane so that it hung between her ears, piling up just above her eyes. He said, "Franca! You are so smart! Tell me what three plus two is!"

His little sister joined in, "Yes! And what is five plus five?"

Franca stopped and bobbed her head up and down at the children, but made no effort to begin counting. The older sister grabbed her little brother by the hand and said to the girl, "Come on. We've no time to fool around. We have to get home, so hurry on."

Franca followed after, trailing behind them as they went through the gates of Turin. The children continued on their way down the main road, but Franca changed her direction. The fresh country air wafted around her as she trotted down the familiar trail. She veered and scampered off, at times bucking and kicking her hind legs at the sky. Franca headed down the dusty path to the west, deep into the beautiful countryside.

Giorgio and Franca were used to traveling in this direction. On Sundays, they had more time to spend together, so they would wander down the wooded trails and find the lush meadow. There, they would enjoy the afternoon, watching the sheep as they grazed. While Giorgio sat in the shade of the broad trees, Franca savored the sweet grass alongside of the sheep. But on this day, as the sun gradually lowered, Franca was alone. Her spirit was filled with disquiet and foreboding. She set upon the field and nipped the sweet clover, jolting her head up after grabbing each mouthful. At this evening hour, there were no sheep to be seen. The shepherd had them rounded up for the night and in the barn for safety's sake. The land outside of the city walls was home to a host of wild creatures. The shepherds especially wanted to protect their flocks from the hungry wolves that roamed the hills.

Danger was in the air. It was new for her to be out without Giorgio near and the surroundings worried her. She grabbed the tufts of grass, glancing from side to side and sprinting in between mouthfuls, and roamed along the easy trail, not paying any attention to where she was going. She was nervous and covered a lot of ground in a short time.

When nightfall first set in, the countryside became full of shadows. But, as the moon rose in the sky, it made the night as bright as midday for her. Even so, it offered her little comfort. The night scents and sounds scared her. She was uneasy, so she kept on trotting. She wandered into a vineyard and stumbled onto a strange and narrow channel. The foliage grew thickly together, acting as a fence on either side of her. The rows of vines were long and kept her from being able to turn to the right or the left. The footpath continued up a smooth hill. When she finally reached the last steps of the vineyard, she was glad to be free of its confinement. She followed the dirt path out of the vineyard and ran west to the main road. Without warning, an owl flew from the dark forest and dove at a mouse. The heavy drumming of its wings spooked her. She whinnied and kicked and raced on ahead.

Never before had she been so frightened. In no time at all, she was lost and covering unfamiliar ground. She did not stop to eat now. Franca just kept running hard. She had lost her sense of direction and so remained on the open, well-trod road. Up and down the hills, she galloped at full speed. Dust and gravel flew up from her hooves. Fallen pine branches that lay on the ground shattered under her pounding feet. She sensed movements in the darkness, and the smell of wolves distressed her. Franca was alone and scared. Every tree, every shadow terrified her. She journeyed over rocky, mountainous country, wherever the open road led her. On and on she ran, always to the west and farther away from Turin.

Giorgio had stayed too late talking with Don Bartolomeo and was surprised when he came out of the rectory. The moon was so high in the sky that he knew he must have been in the parsonage for hours. He looked towards the spot where he had tied Franca, but she was not there. From where he stood, he could see that the lead rope was still tied to the tree. He could not believe that Franca was gone. Certainly, he thought to himself, she could not have gone far. He took hold of the leather strap and saw that it was torn in two. He untied it from the tree, wondering where she would have gone. Giorgio softly called, "Franca, Franca." Talking aloud to himself, he said, "She must have been hungry and headed back to the stable." He slapped the broken strap against his thigh and turned down the narrow passage that led to the square. He ran as fast as he could to the stable. He was so sure that she would be there.

He grabbed the latch of the stable door and burst through. Alessandro stood before him, angry and tired after his day's labor. His blacksmithing apron was covered in soot. His sweat-stained face was still grimy from his work. Giorgio stopped where he stood. He was late for his evening chores, and Alessandro made a point to tell him so.

"Where have you been, boy? The horses here need to be fed and groomed. Have you no concern for our livelihood? No regard for me? These animals belong to others who have paid me well to have them properly cared for." Alessandro spun on his heels as he spoke, reached for a pitchfork, and thrust it into the pile of loose hay. "Get to work! Finish your chores here tonight for tomorrow you will begin work in the smithy. You are forbidden to go to the countryside except for deliveries! It's time you put in a full day's work," roared Alessandro. In his anger, Alessandro did not even notice that Franca was missing. Giorgio did not have the courage to speak to his father and tell him that Franca ran off. It would only make his father more furious at him.

Alessandro marched out of the stable. The door hit hard behind him, bouncing against the old wooden frame. A few moments later, Giorgio heard the door of the inn also bang shut after his father. He knew that if Gemma was still awake, tonight she would hear of his disobedience and forgetfulness. But she would not know that Franca was missing. Giorgio sat on the stable floor and put his head in his hands. With his father's decree, Giorgio was not allowed even to go and look for her. He looked at the horses in the stalls. He did not mean to neglect his chores, and now he had so much work to finish. And taking on work in the hot forge of the smithy was the last thing he wanted.

One of the horses neighed loudly, wrenching him from his thoughts. He went about his chores, giving each animal an armload of hay, and top-dressed each mound with a scoop of oats. After every one of them had fresh water, he grabbed the pitchfork and started cleaning out the stalls. He was tired, and yet he could not rest. There was a beautiful black mare in the stable tonight. He picked up the currycomb and groomed its mane, hoping and praying that Franca would walk through the stable gate. He expected her to come home any minute, but she did not come. He was afraid for his donkey. Where was she? Why did she go? He tried to comfort himself, but it was no use. He prayed, begging God to bring his best friend back to him.

Giorgio finished his work and settled into the straw for the night. He would wait until Franca came. He thought back to the time when he had first held Franca. It was here in this very stable that Giorgio had fed her milk from a leather pouch. She was so weak and sickly during her first winter with him. He hand fed her grain and grass until she was able to take it on her own. The winter months in Turin that year were exceptionally cool, so for that first season, Giorgio made sure that Franca was kept warm in the stable. He covered her with an old woolen blanket during the coldest nights. He covered himself with the same old woolen blanket now, for the night was getting chilly.

Giorgio lay in the stable, and each time he heard a strange noise, he jumped up, thinking Franca had come home. The light of the full moon gleamed like an icy blue beacon in the sky. Giorgio found no comfort in knowing that Franca was somewhere sharing the same moonlight. His heart was breaking. He cried and prayed to God in his loneliness. After a time, he mustered together all of his courage and made plans for the morning. First, he would talk to Aunt Gemma and tell her exactly what had happened. He was sure she would understand. Next, he would go to Don Bartolomeo. As was his routine, he would be saying his Mass before the sun came up. His aunt and his priest would help him. They would know where to start looking for Franca.

6

Two Thieves

Under the same moonlight, in a town many miles away to the west, two thieves were prowling in search of easy plunder. They were willing to steal anything of value and wanted the best they could get their hands on, but the houses on this particular street were places for poor families. The hardworking people of Exilles were sound asleep for the night. It did not take long for the robbers to realize that no jewels or gold or finery of any kind would be found here. Only stone jars and some well-used tools stood leaning up against the dingy walls of the rundown hovels. The first thief, Vincente, wore a heavy cloak that sometimes dragged on the ground. His bulky hat was too big for his head and usually blocked his view. He tripped in the darkness, clumsily bumping into a peasant's cart and nearly falling into it. It creaked and groaned as he pushed it out of his way. From an alley, a dog barked at the noise he had made, so he quickly regained control of himself, adjusted his cape, and continued to move on.

"Hurry up, Martino!" he grumbled under his breath, "What's keeping you? There's nothing here that I want, so let's get out of here and head to a better part of town. Maybe we can find a shopkeeper's door that's been left open."

"Quit bossing me around. I'll be along, just as soon as I gather up something to eat. I'm hungry, that's all," Martino said. He had stopped at the small cart and discovered that it still had some vegetables left over from the day's pickings. Surely, the peasants would not miss this little bit, he thought. In haste, he grabbed all he could get and filled his satchel until he could barely close it. Next, he stashed carrots and onions into his tattered shirt, cinching his belt tighter around his waist to keep all of it from dropping out. It was early in the season, so some of the produce was small, but he did not mind. He was used to taking what he could get. He rubbed his hands over a sugar beet to remove the dirt and took a big bite. It crunched as his teeth sunk into it. Purple juice smeared him on his bearded chin.

"Mmm ... finally, something to eat. This tastes so good," Martino said. The rough years spent warring had not lessened Martino's gratitude for the simple things of life.

Of the two, Vincente was the mean-spirited one. He had no qualms about stealing or lying; in fact, even murder was not above him. He was annoyed and let Martino know it. "Get over here, you buffoon! Eat on your own time. We've only got a few hours to find something worth pilfering, and we've still got to travel to another part of town. Let's move! We'll head towards the square. No doubt there'll be something there for us." With that, Martino rushed to get in step with Vincente, keeping behind him a few paces while still savoring his tasty morsel.

The two men were crude and ignorant of all things beautiful and holy. For years, there had been battles in this region for control of important city-states on the border of France, just east of the Alps. In 1453, the war in this land raged between the French Rene D' Angio and Duke Ludovic of Savoy. The skirmish in Exilles had recently ended, and the members of the army were disbanded without receiving any pay. The men, newly released from military action, took to pillaging here and in other local villages. Vincente and Martino, two discharged soldiers, wanted to be rich to make up for all the years they lost in the war. Vincente put himself in charge and was determined to take whatever his eyes feasted upon, while Martino was content merely to feast. He had no real plans of his own, so he carelessly followed the other man's lead.

As they crept through the city of Exilles in search of their opportunity, they came across a beautiful church. Vincente spoke first, saying to Martino, "Why not begin here? Surely there is plenty of gold and expensive cloth to be had! Maybe silver and some gems as well," he added as he tried the side entrance. "Hey, this door's open. We can easily go in."

Martino was not so readily convinced. As he stood looking at the stalwart church building, he remembered a special day in his childhood. A picture presented itself in his mind. It was of the little church that he and his father went to when he was a young boy, many long years before he had joined the war. It seemed like a lifetime ago. Martino shook himself from the vision. "Vincente," he began, "God's house? Are you sure it is wise?"

"Wise nothing! It's not as if God is here, as if God is watching us. Besides, when was the last time you've even given God a thought — as if you're above thieving. You're the one carrying stolen goods," Vincente pointed out, bristling at Martino's delay. He scoffed, "You and your childish superstitions. No, I'm in command now and you'll do as I say. I bet this place is loaded with treasure, and tonight, it is ours for the taking."

Martino did his best to change Vincente's mind. "But the moon is so bright. Surely someone will see us." As he spoke, Martino stood in the crossroads and looked down the streets in every direction. He hoped for a light, for a noise, for something to distract Vincente from his purpose, but not even the smallest sound escaped from the shops and houses in his view.

"Just get in here," Vincente demanded. Irritated by Martino's stalling, he grabbed him by the arm, and gave him a violent shove towards the open door. "We've still got plenty of time before the morning sun dawns in the sky. Come on. We've got work to do."

Martino removed his rough woolen cap and tucked it into his belt. He tiptoed into the church behind Vincente. They stumbled on the stairs in the darkness, tripping over each other and banging into the old wooden pews. Vincente bumped his face on the edge of one of the side altars and cursed. High above the altar, the moon shone through a round window. It was near to the ceiling and did not offer enough light to guide them. Vincente crawled from

where he had fallen, stood, and stretched out
his arm, angrily ripping a tall candle from its
stand and thrusting it into the sanctuary lamp.
With its gentle flame, he lit a few more candles
and handed one to Martino. Vincente's eyes
blazed when he saw the chalice reflecting back
the light of the fire. For a moment, it seemed to
him a mirror, revealing the deep secrets of his
soul. He stood, knowing that what he intended
to accomplish was an unspeakable crime against
God. The chalice burned in his hands as if it was
fire itself and it slipped from his fingers, crashing
to the stone floor. But he rejected its warning
and greedily turned toward the sacristy.

Martino had entered the church against his
will and now was spooked by the varying shades
of gray caused by the dim lights. Shadows
bounced off the marble altar, making it look
alive. Martino's nerves were on edge, and he was
ready to jump at the next odd occurrence. He
felt sure that they were not alone, sensing that
even the statues were watching them. The look
from the figure of the Blessed Virgin, however,
offered a special tenderness and kindness to him.

Vincente, unlike Martino, remained unshaken,
for he had no regard for this holy place. Vincente
was snooping in the sacristy, opening up every

drawer and grabbing items from the shelves. He
poked his nose in every nook and cranny, becoming more and more agitated all the while. He
jerked open a cabinet door, rummaged through
its contents, and hurled down some old woolen
cassocks. "There," Vincente growled, "this stuff
will serve as a wrapping for the bundle. And here
are some cords so we can tie it all together."

Next, Vincente tossed white albs, beautiful
vestment cloths, and crisp altar linens on the pile.
Some were embroidered with threads of gold
and silver. Martino had thought they would take
just a few small things, but Vincente had bigger
plans. "All of it. Take everything. No one is here
and now is our chance to get our wages for all
those years spent in war. This plunder is ours!"
Vincente exclaimed.

Each closet door was opened one at a time.
If the things inside were of any value whatsoever,
Vincente threw them on the pile of fabrics. In
his rummaging, he discovered a shiny brass key.
He observed it closely. "Well, look at this, Martino. A fancy little key … the bit has the shape
of a cross cut away from it, and its bow looks
like a king's crown. I'll find the lock it goes with
— probably a locked vault, loaded with goods."
He set the key aside.

Martino did his own share of the robbing. He grabbed the gilded candlesticks and the silver patens. The shiny altar bells made a tinkling sound as he tossed them on the growing heap. The eager thieves even stole the silver chalice itself. They came to the tabernacle that was built into the high altar. It was impossible to take. Vincente took one look at the exquisite jewels of its richly embedded framework. With dagger in hand, he gouged at the rubies and sapphires.

"Not enough time to dig these all out. Too bad," Vincente mumbled to himself, shoving his knife back in its sheath. "The tabernacle … is it locked?" Vincente instantly knew the purpose of the little key. "Hustle up, Martino! Fetch that little key or I'll bust this open. No doubt it holds the most valuable treasure."

Martino found the key where Vincente had left it in the sacristy. He extended his arms out for the tabernacle, as if afraid to touch it. It was gilded with gold and ornately decorated. Martino slid the beautiful key into its keyway and unlocked the door. The monstrance was guarded within. In it was a consecrated Eucharistic Host. Martino knew he was doing something terribly wrong. His hesitation made Vincente furious. "You fool!" Vincente bellowed at Martino.

Vincente snatched the monstrance and flung it on the pile. He marveled again at the jewels adorning the tabernacle. His thirst for this world's riches was insatiable. He took hold of his blade again and chipped at the rubies. He would have stayed there until he had removed them all, but the soft glimmer of the morning sun, began warming the few windows that decorated the east side of the church. A faint light glistened on the altar. Even Vincente knew it would soon be time for the early morning Mass. He had worked too hard to risk getting caught in the act now. He put his knife away and extinguished the last glimmering candle, packing it with the other things.

"If we hadn't gotten such a late start all these jewels would be mine, too." Vincente hungrily took one last look around to make sure they had not missed anything else.

Martino needed time to think. His mind was filled with a thousand terrors, and he wanted to run from them all. He stood trembling, with sweat pouring down his face as Vincente bound the cords around the hulking shape. Martino was not as tall as Vincente, but now he stood up to him nose-to-nose in challenge. "All of it? Are you crazy? We can't possibly carry all of it. We can't manage it. It'll slow us down! Leave some of it and take what we can easily haul."

Vincente would not hear of it. He flung Martino out of his way, causing him to stumble into the hard edge of the altar steps. Blood trickled from the back of his head. Vincente paid no attention to his accomplice but instead greedily tied the dark outer fabrics together, concealing the holy things inside. Vincente and Martino dragged the misshapen bundle forward. Finally, Vincente pushed Martino out of the church's door. "Move on, Martino," he threatened. As he forced Martino outside, they rolled down the hard stone steps, tangled up together, and landed on top of their bulging load.

"Get off of me, Vincente! Now what do we do! We've so much loot that together we cannot haul it! We won't be able to get away without being caught," said Martino.

Vincente turned to face Martino and was ready to punch him. He stopped mid-swing when he saw that there, off in the green of the church-yard, a donkey was resting. Poor Franca had run most of the night and finally given up searching for home. She came to the grassy yard of the church and managed to get a few hours of rest. She was lost and looking for anyone to give her some direction. She raised her head and looked up at the two thieves. Vincente approached Franca with his arms waving frantically above his head. She, startled by his hostile advance, shot up and darted from him. "Get over here, Martino, and be quick about it! I've found exactly what we need. Who says God doesn't answer prayers!" Vincente scoffed.

Martino came walking slowly toward Franca. She caught the scent of vegetables and brayed a hopeful "Ee Aw," which this time meant, "Mmm! I smell something tasty! I am hungry!"

Martino, with slow steps, drew near to her. She sniffed at the satchel that now hung over his shoulder. She nudged him in the ribs, hoping to get at the vegetables that he had stashed in his shirt. He felt sorry for her and handed her a red beet. She gladly crunched it, and in one gulp it was gone. Martino soothed Franca as Vincente loaded the bundle of stolen goods on her back. He fastened the unshapely bundle while Martino patted Franca's warm, furry neck.

"Hey Vincente, she likes the vegetables I picked. I think she may even like me. Don't you, my beauty?" Martino said as he turned from Vincente to Franca. With that, Franca nuzzled Martino and obediently followed his lead.

7

Gemma's Kitchen

Before the sun was on the morning horizon, Giorgio met his Aunt Gemma in her kitchen. The pretty violet frock that she wore was dusted with flour. The linen scarf tied around her head hardly managed to keep her long, brown hair away from her face. Her kitchen smelled like a beautiful garden. She turned to greet Giorgio and lightly stepped on the fresh rushes strewn upon the flagstone floor. The scent given off by the strands of lavender mingled with the aroma of her baking, filling the air with the sense of calm and serenity. Her hot oven boasted five loaves of bread and a pan of breakfast pastries. They were fresh out of the oven and lined up on the far edge of her work bench. A woven basket filled with potatoes and onions sat on the floor, as if they were patiently waiting their turn to be used in Gemma's creations. Gemma stood at the table, kneading a fresh batch of dough. Her day's baking and cooking for the customers of the inn was well under way.

"Good morning, Giorgio, you are here early today," Gemma said smiling. She stopped her work and looked closely at him. "Are you feeling ill? You don't look so well this morning." Gemma was the person Giorgio could always count on, so he made no effort to keep anything from her. She understood him through and through. Before Giorgio could say one word, Gemma said, "What is it? Something terrible has happened. Tell me what it is."

Giorgio did all he could do to keep from crying. He had stayed in the stable all night, so his clothes were dingy and still specked with bits of straw. His tired eyes, so filled with worry and sadness, begged for compassion. "It's Franca," Giorgio said. "She's gone. She left me. She's gone and hasn't come back. I waited in the stable for her all night, but she is gone!"

Giorgio fell into Gemma's arms and sobbed. Gemma smoothed his dark, curly hair. Her heart crumbled with every tear he shed. She wanted to cry with him but held her emotions in check, saying, "Sit down here. Tell me the story. How did this happen?"

Giorgio cleared his throat. He rubbed the tears from his face with the cuffs of his shirt and vowed he would not cry anymore. "It happened last night. I tied Franca up, but I stayed too long visiting Don Bartolomeo. It's my fault," he said.

"Franca pulled herself free. By the time I went to get her where I left her tied, she was long gone."

Gemma tried to comfort Giorgio, but he would not have it. He leaned back in his chair, pushing himself away from the table. "When I came to the stable, my father was there, and he was angry — and rightly so. I missed my chores. He was so furious that I didn't dare ask for his help. I didn't have the courage to tell him any- thing about Franca."

Gemma felt a stab in her heart, for she knew how Giorgio loved Franca and how difficult Alessandro could be at times. "My poor boy," Gemma said, "we'll get this straightened out. Franca will come home again. Not to worry, Franca will come home again. In the meantime, here, you have something to eat."

The butter melted into the fresh muffins that Gemma set before Giorgio, but he pushed the plate away. "I will talk with your father. Don't you worry." Gemma reached for Giorgio's satchel and filled it with some fruit and loaves of bread. "Now, Giorgio, you listen to me. You have just enough time to make it to morning Mass. Pray. Believe. Tell Don Bartolomeo what has happened and take any advice he gives you. You will need to go through the city and ask people if they've seen

Franca. And you will have to go to all of your favorite places to see if she is there."

"But Father will not allow it. He is so angry," Giorgio said softly.

"I'll talk with your father. Take this. Here is lunch for you and some fruit and sugar for Franca. And pray while you go on your way."

Giorgio stood up from the table and met Gemma with a gentle embrace. She kissed his cheek tenderly. "Thank you, Aunt Gemma," Giorgio said quietly. "Pray for Franca and me." Giorgio took the satchel and rushed out to St. Silvestro's. The sound of the ringing bells gave him hope.

He was breathless by the time he arrived at the church. Giorgio hurried to be vested as acolyte. As always, Don Bartolomeo was glad when Giorgio entered the sacristy, but the priest said nothing to the boy now. The priest believed silence, when it was appropriate, was holiness. Don Bartolomeo slipped the emerald-colored chasuble over his head and finished vesting for Mass. Giorgio quickly and quietly got himself ready. For Giorgio, the Mass was a moment of simple grandeur. It was like being in Heaven itself. He imagined angels filling the space around the altar and often wondered what the melodies of their hymns of praise really sounded like. Especially in the moments of the consecration, he prayed for his mother and his father, and that the hearts of the townspeople of Turin would turn back to the faith. But today, he could think only of Franca.

When Mass had ended with the final blessing, the small crowd of people shuffled out. One by one, they left the peace offered by St. Silvestro's and reentered the predictable hubbub waiting for them in the town square.

Giorgio faced his priest in the sacristy. He planned to tell him everything, but Don Bartolomeo was the first to speak. "Giorgio, what's wrong? I can see that something grave is on your mind."

Giorgio blurted out his response, holding nothing back. "Something terrible has happened. Franca is missing. It's my fault. She wandered off last night and did not come back to the stable. Now she is lost!" Giorgio held back his tears and boldly added, "I am off to look for her now, but my father has forbidden me to go into the countryside. I am sure that is where she is, so that's where I am going."

"Oh no, Giorgio, not if your father has told you otherwise. You must obey your father's wishes. If he says no going to the countryside, then you must heed his word," the priest said.

"But I am sure that is where she has gone. I've got to go."

"No, Giorgio. I forbid you. Have you talked with your Aunt Gemma?"

"Yes, she knows. She packed me food for the day and told me to search through the city."

"Then, Giorgio, that is what you must do. Go with my blessing." Don Bartolomeo raised his hand, blessing the boy. "Surely, someone has seen her. I'll ask the townspeople when I visit with them in the square this morning."

"Thank you, Father." With that, Giorgio was on his way.

Over the years, Giorgio had explored every street, every little trek in his village. Turin was the only place he had ever lived, so he knew every business place and building site, all of the interesting places, all of the secret spots. Besides that, he and Franca covered so much ground on their regular route, so he was familiar with the farther edges of town. He found it easy to talk with the people and asked everyone he encountered if they had seen Franca. He went to the places she loved best. As he walked, calling for her, he wondered why she did not suddenly appear. He expected her to show up at any moment. Giorgio's faith was being tried like never before. "Why, God? You see her, you know where she is. Bring her back, please, please, bring her back," Giorgio begged. He wondered if God was listening at all. His hope began to fade.

Pietro came running behind Giorgio, hollering and waving his red cap, and at his heels scurried the little dog from the square. Giorgio turned to see them coming, and for a moment, his mood lightened. "So, the pup came back? How is it that he is coming with you?"

"Well, after the chase in the square, my father set me to work washing out the blue silk scarf, but he decided that the silk was too fine and so had me set it aside and do some other task. A few hours after the chase in the square, the dog came and sniffed it out. He sat next to it, as if he was sorry for ruining it. My father felt sorry for the creature, and so now he is my pet. He really is a good dog. I wanted to name him something noble, like Marcus or Caesar, but my father calls him Rascal, so that is his name."

Giorgio smiled. He could see that Rascal was just right for Pietro, and he was happy for him, but he could not help it. His heart grieved at the loss of his own pet. Pietro shared Giorgio's sadness.

"Giorgio, any sign of her? Have you found her yet? Don Bartolomeo told my father about Franca. My father has given me permission to help look for her."

"Pietro, I feel as if I've searched in every place. Maybe you have some good ideas?"

"Did you climb to the top of the hill? We can see most of everything from there — the business in the square and even the main road that leads out of town."

Together, they started the long climb up to the highest point in Turin. Rascal ran on ahead of them, as if he knew who they were looking for. They sat down near each other on the hill-top, in the shade given by a big boulder. "Here, we can see everything," Pietro said.

Butterflies fluttered by them, but they hardly took notice. On any other day, they would have made a tournament out of chasing them, but today the boys talked little. They were keenly focused on the view below them. When they looked straight ahead, they could see the activity of the merchants at the shops. If they looked to the right, most of the main road was in plain sight. Only a few clusters of trees and the crests of smaller hills blocked the scene. They watched for a long time without saying a word to each other. The breeze carried to them the song of the *Angelus* bells, breaking into the silence that wrapped around them. It was the noon hour. Together they prayed.

"Hungry?" Giorgio said to Pietro, who was scooting himself closer to Giorgio.

"Yes! Anything will do." Rascal appeared from the shrubbery and settled himself next to Pietro, patiently waiting for a handout.

Giorgio emptied the satchel of the bread and fruit, but put the sugar lumps back. The Latin prayer book tumbled out with the other things. In the excitement of the night, he had forgotten all about it. Pietro noticed it and smiled a little. "Giorgio," he said slowly, "there's something I have to tell you. It is both good news and bad news. This morning my father talked with Don Bartolomeo. That's what I was running to tell you about, but when I heard that you were out searching for Franca, it must have slipped my mind." Pietro paused for a moment and looked into Giorgio's eyes. "Anyway, together they are set on finding a monastery school for me. I'll stay in Turin for a few years yet and continue preparing, and then I'm off." Pietro was not sure if he should be happy or sad, for he did not know how Giorgio would take his news. Maybe it would prove to be too much for him, losing two friends in one day.

Giorgio smiled back at his friend. "Who knows," he said, "maybe you'll become a cardinal one day. You're used to wearing a red cap." Pietro was relieved and smiled happily.

Giorgio stood up and surveyed the land below them. The shady place where they had been sitting was not any more comfortable than being in the sun. Together, they headed up the slope to a cooler spot in a grove of trees, where Rascal was crazily digging a hole. He was determined to unearth whatever poor creature was hiding there. The two boys climbed a tall pine tree and found comfortable spots in the branches, relaxing in the breeze that entertained the boughs around them. They intentionally faced different directions so that each would have a slightly different view, and they kept their eyes on the scene below them. Hours passed with no sign of Franca.

Giorgio looked down at the city spread out before him. Today had given him plenty of time to think, and as much as a young boy could, he tried to understand the questions that bothered him. "Why did Franca go? Why is my father always angry? Why are the people of Turin so discouraged?" In that moment, Giorgio realized that he was a lot like the rest of the townsfolk. He must not give up hope. The talks he had had with Aunt Gemma and Don Bartolomeo ran through his mind. Deep down, his father was a good man, and Giorgio knew that as a son, he had a responsibility towards his father. Before he had left early this morning in search of Franca, he had fed and watered the animals in the stable, but by now they would need to be tended to. He made a resolve that from now on, he would be more obedient and take his chores seriously. It was time he grew up.

"Now I understand, Pietro, that it is easy to lose heart: when life is hard, when things don't go as one wants them to. Franca is gone, and I am so lonely. I understand now how my father must feel. Maybe he is sad and lonely, too." Giorgio looked at the world around him and high up into the azure dome which crowned it. "Please, please bring Franca back home," Giorgio prayed.

8

Giorgio's Father

Gemma listened and prayed as the noon *Angelus* bells chimed. Giorgio had been gone for long hours, and she was curious to know if he had found Franca. She had finished her baking for the day and was well into preparing food for the next meal. She gathered the used baking pans and bowls and set them in a tub filled with soapy water. The brick oven always made the kitchen warm, but today it seemed unbearable to her. She sat at the bench and put her feet up on a low stool, sipping her cup of cool mint tea and turning over in her mind the things she meant to tell Alessandro. Her mind travelled back to the days when they were children. She remembered him as a boy. He was as happy and as rambunctious as all the other boys his age in Turin. Together, they would have mock battles in the city square. Some of the boys claimed to be vandals, come to conquer Turin and its surrounding territory. They would clang and clatter their homemade weapons and shout at each other. The vendors would come out of their small shops and send them away. The boys would gather their arms and race out of the city square and into the countryside to continue their games.

Gemma had great affection and admiration for her brother. During the years of their father's illness, Alessandro became responsible for Gemma and their aging parents. He did double time in the smithy, and his skill increased. His rapport with the men of the village developed. They now respected Alessandro in his own right and appreciated the quality of his workmanship. He was efficient and quick to supply their needs. During those days, Gemma took care of her father and helped in the inn. Their father's illness went on for two years, and he quietly passed from this world in the cool winter. Their mother was exhausted with managing both businesses and the steady care of her husband. In the spring, when the world was just waking up from winter's sleep, she also passed away. This left Alessandro as head of the household. Gemma and he worked hard to keep their parents' legacy thriving.

She sipped her tea, letting her memory present an image of Alessandro and his wife, and of her mother and father. Perhaps the loss of three loved ones in such a short span of time was more than he could bear.

Alessandro and Maria were happy together. They had each other and looked forward to their first — and only — child. But Maria became weak, and the day of Giorgio's birth proved too hard for her. After Giorgio was born, her condition became worse. In a matter of two short weeks, she died, leaving Alessandro brokenhearted and with a new baby to care for. Gemma remembered the scene. The details were etched in her mind. Together Gemma and Alessandro stood in the room. Gemma held the baby Giorgio, and Alessandro knelt by his wife's bed. He held her hand until she breathed her last breath. The room was silent.

Gemma let go of her deep thoughts when Alessandro came through the door. He entered into her kitchen and sat himself at the table. His clothes reeked with the smell of metal and smoke. He had finished his morning's work and was tired and dirty. Wiping his grimy face and hands with a cotton cloth, he asked, "Where is Giorgio? I have yet to see him today." He rested his head in his hands for a moment and then reached for some fresh bread. He cut himself a thick slice. The golden crust crumbled under the knife, presenting the soft interior of the loaf. It melted in his mouth. He sat back in his chair, thankful for both the bread and the break from his work.

Since she had let Giorgio go early this morning, leaving him free from kitchen chores, Gemma had extra work to do. She was not only weary from her work but concerned for Giorgio. She got up from her chair and adjusted her apron, ready now to speak with Alessandro. She ladled soup into a bowl and brought it to her brother. "Giorgio is gone," she said sternly. "He came in early today to say that Franca is missing. I gave him permission to go out searching for her."

Alessandro looked up in disbelief. "What is this? It's the first I've heard of it. They were in the stable last night, so what has happened?" Alessandro asked. His big arms rested on the table. This was news to him, and he expected the full story.

Gemma stood straight with her shoulders squared and her arms folded across her apron. She spoke firmly to Alessandro. "No, they were not in the stable last night. At least, Franca was not. Only Giorgio. And if you would have greeted him as a father should greet his son, he would have told you the story himself," Gemma said.

"What story? What has happened? How long has Franca been missing?"

Gemma brushed her hair from her eyes and set a plate of cheese before him. She wiped her hands on her apron and looked at Alessandro. She respected Alessandro very much and although she felt pity for him, today she raised her voice.

"What is the matter with you? Have you nothing to be thankful for? This house, your work, our beautiful city? Giorgio? How can you stay so heartless?"

"What do I have to do with any of this? I've done my best with the boy."

Gemma faced her brother once more. "You have let yourself become rough and angry. You've forgotten the simple things of life. So focused on making a living that you've lost sight of what life means. Always you say, 'So much work to do' ... you have lost the hope that comes with Sunday, the day to pause and pray ... allowed yourself to lose faith, to become slack in the practice of the old ways, the true ways. When was the last time you spent time with Giorgio, talked with him, laughed with him? You are missing out, but worse than that, you are blaming him." The words poured out from her, and they were not easy for Alessandro to take.

For once, Alessandro was silent. He looked up at his sister, knowing that what she had said of him was true. He took to heart her words and asked himself some hard questions. Had he been blaming Giorgio all these years? Had he been taking his son for granted? He had not thought this way before now. Alessandro sat quietly for a few minutes more and then got up from the chair and went to the door. "I'm going to look for him," he said, "I'll talk to him and help him search for Franca. She can't be far. She loves the boy and will find her way home." With that, Alessandro hurried out.

At the same time, Giorgio and Pietro were making their way down from the top of the hill. They hesitated in every place that offered a fresh view. Whenever the two boys stopped, Rascal soon appeared, abandoning his own expedition to join in theirs. There, they would stand for a few moments to look out at the world around them, always hoping for any signs of Franca. The summer breeze was warm and made the boughs of the pines bounce noiselessly. They were thankful that the scorching heat of the day was coming to an end as they hiked down the hill and into the square. They separated at the city gate, with Pietro and Rascal turning to the right.

They were going to the tailor shop to share the morning's adventure with Pietro's father, while Giorgio headed straight away to St. Silvestro's. He would have to tell Don Bartolomeo that he had no luck in finding Franca. As he passed groups of people about their business, friends called to him, "Any sign of her? Have you found her yet?" Giorgio shook his head no, but he felt a little better knowing that they cared.

"We'll keep an eye out for her, Giorgio. She will be found, don't you worry."

By this time, Giorgio's father had been searching for both Giorgio and Franca ever since he had left Gemma's kitchen a few hours earlier. Alessandro had walked alone and had had uninterrupted time to consider his ways. He had realized that he must put things in order, admit his hardheartedness, and change his brusque ways. At length, his heart felt the peace that only God can give.

Alessandro regarded the people bustling around him. He stood head and shoulders above the average man of Turin, and so his eyes easily scanned the entire courtyard. He was relieved when he discovered Giorgio nearing the center of the crowded square. In haste, he dodged around a close-knit group of men talking and laughing together. Alessandro quickened his pace and ran to meet Giorgio.

Giorgio looked up and through the crowd he could see his father towering above the others and coming toward him. He panicked a little and wondered to himself what would he say? And why was his father moving so fast to him? Alessandro was a big man, and a few of his long strides covered a lot of ground. He is still angry. I'm sure I'm in trouble," Giorgio thought to himself. He hung his head and walked on to meet his father. Giorgio realized he would have to explain everything.

When they met, Alessandro spoke first. "Giorgio, Gemma told me what has happened," he said, "I'm sorry, Giorgio. I was so wrapped up in myself that I didn't even notice that Franca was gone. I should have listened to you last night ... should have helped you search for her. I'm sorry for not being there to help you. Please forgive me."

Giorgio looked at his father. He stood in his father's shadow, for the afternoon sun was behind him. Shafts of light glinted on his hair and clothing. Giorgio did not know what to make of it. Was this an apology coming from his father? Maybe Giorgio did not hear it right, he was so worn out from lack of sleep and the weariness that comes with worrying. Giorgio said plainly, "Franca's gone and hasn't come back. She should be back by now. I don't have a clue as to where she might be. She's lost and it's all my fault."

"No, I am the one to blame. Please forgive me, Giorgio. I should have let you explain yourself last night. I'm to blame for so many things, but today I am making a new start."

"What do you mean?" Giorgio asked.

"I want to be happy again Giorgio. I want the two of us to get along as a father and son should," Alessandro said. "I've been unkind and now am so sorry."

Giorgio just stood there. "Could this be true?" he wondered. But Giorgio could see that there was something different about his father.

His father asked, "Are you heading to talk with Don Bartolomeo?"

"Yes, I thought I would go into the church and see if he is there. I wanted to tell him that I am giving up on finding Franca."

"No, Giorgio. We mustn't ever give up. We've only begun searching for her, and we will keep on looking until we find her. She is a smart little donkey and able to take care of herself. She'll come back home, just you wait and see." Alessandro put his hand easily on Giorgio's shoulder and continued, "I haven't been to church since your mother's funeral. I just couldn't bear it. But today, I realized that I cannot live in the past. I cannot hold this sorrow anymore." Alessandro reached out for Giorgio and drew him close. Giorgio put his arms around his father's waist.

Alessandro laughed a little and said, "Is it okay if I come to the church with you? It's been such a long time for me and I'm a bit hesitant. Don Bartolomeo won't throw me out if I walk in with you, will he?"

Giorgio had to smile at the picture of Don Bartolomeo, a medium-sized man, trying to throw his father, the mighty blacksmith, out of the church. "No, I don't think Don Bartolomeo would try to throw you out, but I know for a fact that he couldn't!" he said, grinning happily.

Alessandro put his arm across Giorgio's shoulder. Together, they walked across the square. People greeted them in passing with questions about Franca and if she'd been found yet. When they entered St. Silvestro's, Don Bartolomeo saw them there and thanked God for this miracle. He was glad to see father and son reconciled. Giorgio and his father knelt and prayed for a while, then quietly went to the vestibule, where Don Bartolomeo stood waiting for them. The three of them talked together for a long while, standing outside in front of the church. While they told the priest of the day's adventure, he could see that their relationship had been healed. Alessandro's heart filled with happiness that day. He had a new appreciation for Giorgio and for Don Bartolomeo. Alessandro had found peace and felt the love of God.

9

The Way Home

Franca was not in a happy mood. She had roamed all night and had little chance to rest in the churchyard before Vincente and Martino spied her. Now, she was heading back the same way that she came. She missed her daily routine. Giorgio had always made sure that the cart she usually pulled was never overloaded. Not once had he worked her to the point of exhaustion as she was being worked now. It was obvious that Vincente had no care for her. To him, she was needed only to make his way easier. The load on her back was almost more than she could carry. It wobbled from side to side, especially when she was on sloping terrain. She had a hard time managing, for her body had not had a chance to recover from her long run the night before. She was hungry and thirsty. She missed the comfort of the stable, but most of all she missed Giorgio.

To make matters worse, her company was gloomy. Vincente was angry and when he spoke, it was only to complain to Martino. He grumbled about the heat of the sun and about the crooked trail and about how they were not getting far enough fast enough. He would slap Martino with his broad hat if Franca went too slow, which made Franca veer off course and just wasted more time. Vincente grouched again if Franca went too fast, especially if her quick steps made the bundle shift.

Martino was not like Vincente. He was quiet most of the time. He was not feeling good about stealing from the church, and he was getting tired of Vincente bossing him around. This journey was hard for Martino, but it was good for him, too. He had plenty of time to rethink his actions. When Vincente was out of earshot, Martino would confide to Franca how he felt about his misdeeds. "Little donkey, I've done something awful, and I've got to find a way to make up for it. But for now, I'll see to it that you are safe. I'll take care of you."

Without knowing it, Martino talked to her just like Giorgio did. She sometimes snickered back to him, convincing Martino that she was really listening to him and comprehending all that he was saying. He patted her neck and rubbed his hand over her smooth jaw as they walked along.

Vincente complained, "Stupid donkey! Can't you go any faster! We've got to keep moving. We are halfway there. We need to make it to Turin before nightfall."

"All the way to Turin ... are you sure? And what's our hurry, I'd like to know?" Martino asked.

"We need to get rid of this loot before word spreads. We've got to sell this stuff to the first interested buyer and that means getting to a big city like Turin. The square will be full of people, like merchants and tradesmen. There will be a buyer there, I'm sure of it. Turin, that's the next town, you stupid fool. Once our job is done there, we can each take our share and go our separate ways. I, for one, am tired of your company."

Vincente continued forcing them on ahead. He gave Franca no time to rest and little chance to grab the meadow grasses as she walked by. Franca trudged along, feeling the heavy burden of the pack on her back, but she was a resilient animal and brave of heart. She would keep going for Martino's sake.

Martino patted Franca's neck, talking sweetly to her. "Where do you come from, little donkey? Surely you have a home, and someone is missing you. From the looks of you, you are used to doing your share of work." Martino reached down as he walked, pulled some tall

grasses out, and fed them to Franca as they plod-
ded along. Franca sniggered and greedily ate the
greenery with delight. "Like it?" Martino asked
as he reached for more blades of grass. He kept
talking soothingly to her, saying, "When I was a
young boy, my father had a donkey just like you
that he called Bruno. I remember Papa hitching
him to the grain mill, and there Bruno would
spend part of the morning walking in endless
circles. He carried water from the well, too, and
also delivered sacks of grain and other supplies
up into the mountains for the shepherds tending
their flocks there."

Martino looked kindly at Franca and saw that
she was working too hard. He turned and spoke
to Vincente saying, "This pack is too much for
her: the weight is not balanced, and the whole
bundle is lopsided. Can't we stop and adjust it?
Maybe lighten the load a bit," Martino begged.
"Besides, we've been moving steadily since before
sun up. We have covered a lot of ground."

Vincente spat on the ground and grumbled,
"There's no chance of stopping now, Martino!
We're going to keep moving."

"We're far enough away from Exilles. We've
long since left the main road and so are safe
from being discovered. Going cross-country on

the footpaths has kept us from being spotted by everyone except the birds. Besides, my feet ache," Martino said. He shuffled his feet a little to prove his point. He was doing his best to get Vincente to take a break so that Franca could rest.

"You fool! You keep moving, or it'll be more than your feet that are sore!" Vincente growled. Again, he slapped Martino with his hat. Franca jumped off the trail, and Vincente bellowed at her. He picked up a dead tree limb from the ground and shook it at Martino. "Next time, I'll use this instead."

Martino coaxed Franca back to the trail and walked along with her. "I'm sorry, little friend," he said. "I tried. At least we have each other, right?" Martino gathered more grass for Franca to nibble.

Time passed slowly. Everywhere he looked, Martino saw woodlands and meadow and hills. The route they were on curved up and down rises and under copses of trees and around large rocks. Together, the trio hiked on. Martino frequently had to reach up and support the bundle to keep it from sliding off of Franca's back. Sometimes, the lumpy, hard things that were stowed in it poked Franca's sides. The load was becoming more and more uncomfortable for her. Every few miles, the contents of the load would rearrange and begin to slip off. The things in the pack clanked as she walked. It was easy to spot the shape of the candlesticks poking up under the fabric covering. From the looks of it, all of the metal articles had worked their way out of the center of the bundle and were now barely contained in the outer edges of the pack. Vincente turned and saw the bundle sliding. "Protect that load, Martino," he commanded.

Martino gladly brought Franca to a halt. "The sun is getting high. The animal needs to rest. I need to rest," Martino said.

"We'll stop for a few minutes, but that's it," Vincente said. He was sweating under his heavy cloak and also was exhausted, though he would not admit it to Martino. "We've got to make it to Turin. We're well over halfway there," he said, but Martino was no longer listening to him.

They stopped in a clearing near a small brook. The wild cherry trees that grew there were loaded with fruit. Tall meadow grass grew in luscious clumps, and red raspberries were within view, growing just on the edge of the dell. Franca was relieved to stop walking. She greedily ate the tall grass and ambled to the edge of the brook for a cool drink.

"Hold steady now, my little friend," Martino said. He loosened the pack from Franca's back and as he put his hand on the coarse ropes that went around the pack and under Franca's white belly, he saw that the ropes had burned through her hide. The cords were damp. Only then did he discover that she was bleeding.

Now it was Martino's turn to vent his anger. Frantically, he undid the bloodied ropes and held them up for Vincente to see. "Vincente! You've

pushed her too far. She needs some doctoring."
He finished untying all of the knots. The whole
bundle slid off, without any help from Martino,
and landed in the soft meadow grass. A small,
golden crucifix fell out, tumbling down the slope
for a short way. Martino stooped to pick it up.

Vincente was furious. "What are you doing,
you fool!" He stretched out his walking stick and
swung it at Martino.

"Oh, no, you don't!" Martino grabbed the
stick with both hands and shoved Vincente down
onto the stony path. "This donkey is cut. She
needs proper care. We are not going anywhere
until I can help her."

For the first time, Vincente said nothing.
He had felt Martino's strength and knew he
meant what he said. Vincente got up off the
rocky soil and brushed the dust and debris from
his clothes. "Fine, you tend to her, then," was
all he said.

It was not easy for him to do, but Vincente
managed to drag the bundle to a nearby tree.
He made several trips back and forth, grabbing
up every bit of the stolen goods and shoving
the smaller tokens into his pouch. When he was
satisfied, he sat himself down in the shade, leaned
his head back, and shut his eyes, pretending to rest.

Martino set to work. He rushed into the underbrush, searching for the leaves of some healing plants. Instead, he found a thick growth of moss on an old, rotting log. He tore it off from where it grew. He brought huge clumps of it to where Franca stood. Her entire body was soaked with sweat. Lathered foam collected on her haunches.

"I hope this will bring you some comfort," Martino said kindly. "It'll at least be a layer of padding between your sores and the rope. This is the last leg of the journey, little donkey, then you will be free."

Vincente got up and dragged the bundle to Martino. Together, they set it up again on Franca's back. Vincente held the load in place while Martino managed to bind the ropes with care. Martino worked as gingerly as he could, packing thick layers of moss over the gashes in her hide. Some of the cuts were deep, but most of the bleeding had stopped. He wanted to be sure that the ropes no longer hurt her and so positioned them away from the most tender areas.

"There, that should help, little donkey," Martino said. He urged Franca on, but when she took her first step, the huge pack shifted. The

silver patens fell out of the bundle and clanged as
they landed against a hard rock.

Vincente watched it all happen, and his anger
mounted. "You buffoon! You and your stupid
donkey! Pick that stuff up." Vincente raised his
walking stick to smack Franca with it. Martino
got in front of Vincente and grabbed the stick.

"No you don't! Let the creature be!" Martino said. Franca sidestepped out of range, jog-
ging off the path. She stood near a thicket of
berries and started sniffing. She nipped at some
of the tender shoots.

Vincente shoved Martino to the ground
and raised the stick against him. Martino got up
quickly and pushed him away. "Don't hit her!
She's just a little donkey, and you've put way too
much on her. She's stiff and sore." Martino tried
to sound reasonable. "Besides, we lose everything if we lose her," he said. He knew Vincente
would not like that to happen and would make
an attempt to hold his temper. Besides, Vincente
was finding out that Martino, when convinced
that he was doing the right thing, could easily
overpower him. He had no choice but to follow
Martino's order.

Together, they repacked the fallen articles
and set out to accomplish their journey. When-

ever Franca balked, Vincente would threaten to beat her again, but he did not raise his stick or his hand. Martino gave her the last carrot from his satchel. Slowly, they covered the miles together. It was now midafternoon.

Vincente wanted to regain control and so yelled once more at Martino. "We part ways in Turin tonight, Martino. I won't need you anymore."

"And what of the donkey? What happens to her?" Martino asked.

"Who cares! There won't be much left of her after today. She can be on her own as far as I'm concerned. All she has to do is to make it to Turin tonight."

Martino saw that some moss was falling out of place. He brought Franca to a halt to reposition it. "Little friend, don't worry. I'll find someone to take care of you." Franca snuffled and wagged her head up and down.

10

Piazza di Grano

Franca sniffed the familiar smells in the air and sensed that she was drawing closer to home. She saw the flock of sheep on a near hill, happily grazing, and so picked up her pace. She did her best to trot, but could only hobble. Her front leg sent stinging pains up to her shoulder. She was limping but Martino could not get her to slow down. As her steps quickened, bunches of moss fell from where they were stuffed under the rope. The cords loosened and slipped back and forth over her skin. Her old wounds tore open and bled all over again, but she refused to feel the pain. She had only one thing on her mind now: she had to find Giorgio. She picked up speed, and as she did, the heavy, awkward pack shifted. It jostled to and fro. The rope needed to be refastened, but she would not slow down.

Once more Vincente's anger mounted. "There she goes again! Every time we come to a downward slope she goes faster. Settle that beast down! Get her to walk smooth and steady. Settle her down, Martino, or I will!" Vincente threatened.

"Now what's the problem? She's moving, isn't she, and in the right direction. You should be happy because now Turin is in sight," Martino said.

"Don't get smart with me, you buffoon. I can see the gates of the town from here. Less than a mile to go, but we don't need the goods being damaged because now the stupid little donkey is in the mood to run! Besides, I'm tired. The town's in sight, so we can keep a fair pace. We've made good time."

Martino grabbed Franca's lead rope and worked to settle her down. "Come on, little donkey, no need to hurry now. Go easy or you'll deepen your wounds. You've got a sore leg, and it'll only get worse if you force yourself onwards. You are a valiant little donkey, and I am sorry that I can't stop to care for you now, but I promise in Turin everything will be all right. I'll take you to the stable and tend to you there. I'll make sure you get water and something to eat. I'll wipe you down and put healing salve on your wounds. Just settle down a bit so that you don't hurt yourself."

Martino held Franca steady and rubbed her fetlock. He wished he could do something for her. He was sorry that they were no longer near the small creek, for he was sure that the

cool water would ease some of her pain. Her leg
was beginning to swell. Martino wanted to get
Vincente's attention away from Franca. He did
not want this little donkey to get beaten, so he
decided to humor Vincente.

"Well, what are your plans for when we get
to Turin?" he asked. "Do you know the names
of any buyers in that town? Any ideas of where
to go first?" Martino had Franca walking in slow,
measured steps. His questions worked magic on
Vincente.

Vincente straightened his posture, now
walking tall with gentlemanlike steps. He became
more businesslike and let himself slip into deep
thoughts. "I figure it's best if we could make it
to the town square. That's the place where most
of the people will be gathered. Someone there
will have enough sense to know what this bundle is worth. There must be traders there who'd
be interested in the gold and silver goblets. All
of that stuff can be melted down, and the gems
can be separated. The fabrics can be remade into
other garments. Maybe the tailor would like
those. Or maybe a merchant would be willing to
buy the whole lot for a good price. That would
be the easiest, quickest way." Vincente raised
his eyes and scrutinized the clouds above him.

In his mind, he counted his profits. His dreams unraveled like the thread from his tattered cape, unwinding, with one thought leading into the next. He looked around him, and instead of seeing trees and meadows he saw riches and endless treasures. Yes, he would finally be a rich man. He saw himself dressed in the finest apparel. A stylish hat on his head would display a long, black, ostrich plume. He would walk with his head high, and the common folk would whisper as he strode by them. Finally, Vincente thought, the world would be at his feet.

Martino noticed the change in Vincente's demeanor. His dreaming had affected his stride. Martino chuckled softly at the sight of Vincente walking in elegant fashion, as if his dreams were his reality. It was important to Martino to keep Vincente calm so that he would continue his leisurely stroll, affording Franca more time to rest. "Sounds as if you've thought this whole thing through," Martino spoke softly, in order to keep Vincente in his dreamlike state.

"Oh, I've thought it through all right." He looked over his shoulder, glancing back at Martino. "I'll sell the whole lot to the first man that makes a fair deal with me, and then I'll be set for life." Vincente smiled at his own cleverness.

"That sounds like a good plan," Martino offered, but he did not want any part of it for himself.

"No more soldiering for me, Martino. I'll trade some gold for a beauty of a horse, and a fast one at that, and I'll ride in style. I'll gather all of the gear I need, a fine suit of clothes, and a sharp sword, and then it's off to Genoa for me." His imagination stretched out before him in an endless vision. Vincente's mind was wandering, thinking of all the possibilities that were in store for him. He saw himself as a conqueror, a genius, a tough and mighty man. "Maybe I'll get myself a ship and sail the trade routes. I could take up pirating," he said. Vincente was becoming more and more arrogant and thinking himself invincible. "Yes, that's it. I'll be forever rich, forever in charge, making my own way by my own rules." He rubbed his greedy hands together.

Vincente's talk made Martino sick at heart. By now, Martino was fed up with this whole adventure. He was sorry that he had taken any part in it. It had not been his idea to rob a church or to take more than they could haul on their own or to burden this little donkey in the process. He looked at Franca, laboring under the load on her back. Sweat ran down from her neck and covered her shoulders. Her limp had worsened. She was bloodied and bruised. Seeing her in this way while Vincente talked on and on about how great he was made Martino angry. Fury boiled up within him. He shouted at Vincente, "I'm tired of being bullied, Vincente. I've had it with you! I'm done with wars and fighting. I'm done with thieving and running. When we arrive in Turin, I'm turning myself in. This kind of life is no life."

Vincente stopped in his tracks and stared at Martino. "You're crazy," he said, jolted from his dream. "You're a crazy fool. This stuff will make each of us rich, but it's all right with me if you give yourself up. I'll gladly take your share. Live in luxury, that's what I aim to do. I'll never want for anything ever again. Run my own life, go where I please. I'll be free!"

"You think that is freedom? No, it's not for me; it's not the kind of life I want. I will not have it. Forever being on the run, hiding out, always in fear of being caught, and most of all forever knowing I've done something horrible. It's not for me," he said.

As he walked on, Martino's hand rested on the burden on Franca's back. His mind took him back to his childhood: to his work in his father's gristmill and to the happy days they had together. He considered how disappointed his papa would feel if he knew how he was living today and of the serious crime he had committed.

"Go ahead, all the more for me!" Vincente barked back at him. "Just make sure you put plenty of distance between you and me and don't be reporting me to the law. All I need is a couple of weeks and I'm bound for the sea. No one will catch me there," Vincente said.

"Bah! You're the fool. Go ahead and do what you've always done. You do just what you see fit — anything to please yourself. But for me, I'm heading for a church, confessing to a priest, and facing up to my crimes. I aim to take my just punishments."

"No way, Martino, not for me, I'm moving on. I'm heading to paradise."

"You can't be sane. Paradise? That's where you're mistaken. No, it's me who will be free," Martino said.

Martino felt good about what he had made up his mind to do, even though he knew it would be hard. He also knew it would mean he'd have to deal with the law and serve his time in prison. That is, unless the judge was merciful to him. He turned to Franca and patted her kindly. This had been a long day. Since its early start before dawn, Martino and Franca had become true friends. Franca trusted Martino, and this made him feel good. He had earned her friendship by saving her from Vincente's anger and taking care of her, and now it was time he made friends with God. As a young boy, his papa had taught him right from wrong. Why did he choose to stray from his father's teaching? He looked around at the countryside that surrounded him, in search of the answer. The late-afternoon sun bathed the way in front of him in warmth and light.

Franca raised her head and sniffed the air. She was beginning to realize how close to home she was. She recognized the landscape and knew that she was now not only in familiar territory, but in one she loved most. The scents and sounds thrilled her. She walked, wagging her head from side to side and plodding through the meadow where she and Giorgio would spend their lazy Sundays together. Giorgio was on her mind. She stopped at the tree where Giorgio always sat. She pawed at the ground, but Martino nudged her forward. She missed Giorgio and his kindness to her. She longed for her cozy place in the stable. She remembered the carrots and the apples, and suddenly she got so excited thinking of it all that without warning, she let out such a loud bray that both Vincente and Martino were caught off-guard. Vincente was walking three steps ahead of Franca, and when she sounded off, he nearly jumped out of his skin. He bumbled from the path, tripped over his own feet, and rolled down a small hill, landing in a thistle bush. The pickers stuck to his clothes and pierced his skin. He had a hard time getting up on his own, but Martino offered him no aid.

"Now what's the matter with that donkey? Is she crazy?" Vincente yelled to Martino.

"Just leave her alone. She's probably worn out from traveling. Let her rest here in the meadow for just a little while. We're so close to town. Let the donkey rest. We can carry the goods into the square without her help," Martino pleaded.

"No, we'll have none of that. All she has to do is get us to the square to a buyer, and then she's free."

This time, Franca looked right at Vincente and twisted her mouth so that her lower jaw was as far to the left as her upper jaw was to the right. She brayed, "Ee aw! Ee aw! Ee aw!" as loudly as she could. Vincente, convinced that the animal had gone mad, stepped off to the side faster than he thought possible. She picked up her trot again. Now, she was on the dusty road that led directly to the town square. In a few short minutes, she would be in the *piazza* and in sight of the stable. All of the sights and sounds were well-known to her. She was coming home.

11

The Miracle

The sound of Franca's hooves clattered lightly on the cobblestone as she passed through the gates. Even at this distance, she could smell the fruit and vegetables in the various stands in the market square. She was staggering now, but she continued on. At the sight of the fountain, her steps quickened. She was so thirsty, and the sweet taste of the cool fountain water would revive her.

Martino did his best to slow her down, but she would not. Instead, Martino walked alongside her, guiding her with one hand on her halter while stroking her neck with the other. Her steps had become uneven, and her front shoulder lowered each time she moved forward. The awkward bundle shifted. It tipped to her right side and the ropes loosened even more. Martino got hold of the cord to steady the load one more time and jerked Franca to a halt. Her duty to Vincente was nearly accomplished, and Martino wanted no more harm to come to her.

"Vincente, hold the donkey back while I go and fetch her some water. Otherwise she's likely to run into the crowd of people just to get to the fountain."

Vincente was grouchy and tired from traveling through the night and for the whole day. His ragged leather hat sat at an angle across his head, and he leaned on his walking stick as he went along. His dreams egged him on. He had his fill of this adventure and was impatient to start living his own. Vincente heard what Martino said but did not respond. He had no concern for the beast. They walked around the outer edges of the square because it was full of so many townsfolk. The place was a bustle of activity, for the vendors were closing up their shops for the evening. Small groups of men helped one another taking down their makeshift booths.

Vincente was trailing ten steps behind Franca. His stick clacked against the cobblestone as he walked. He was entranced by his thoughts of wealth. He looked around the square for a likely buyer, and as he did so, he caught a glimpse of Franca's load tipping. The bulky heap leaned heavily to one side and in a few moments would hit the ground. Vincente became enraged at the sight of it sliding off. They had finally arrived in Turin, and he was not about to lose his prize now. Like a crazy man, he ran to the donkey with his stick raised in the air.

Martino screamed at him, "Vincente, no! Spare the animal! We are here now. She has played her part well enough."

Vincente was in a frenzy. His eyes burned with rage and as he charged at Franca, spit flew from his mouth followed by an unrecognizable sound. "Arh!" he bellowed, waving his cane high in the air. He rushed at Franca and set upon clubbing her.

Martino held his hands up in an effort to protect Franca from the blows. "Vincente, stop! If not for her sake, for yours! You'll draw too much attention!" But Vincente was beyond being reasonable. He aimed to kill her. Vincente had had enough of the little donkey being in command. He lunged at the wounded animal. "This little beast has to learn a lesson," Vincente shouted as he let his rod come down hard on her neck. Franca felt the blow and for a moment seemed about to fall.

Martino stood in between Vincente and Franca and charged ahead, intending to grab him around his middle and pull him off balance. Vincente pushed him violently out of the way and continued beating Franca. Knowing that she was home gave her renewed determination. She fearlessly kicked at Vincente. Her powerful legs and sharp hooves connected with their target. He doubled over, holding his broken ribs.

"Ahh!" he screamed. "I'll destroy the little beast!" With one arm folded across his rib cage, he picked up the rod and whipped Franca's head again and again.

The people in the square were drawn by the clamorous tumult and gathered around, but they did not immediately step forward to help the donkey. The man with the stick was out of his mind. For a long moment, they all stood staring at the incredulous scene. They could see that the animal was exhausted and bleeding where the ropes had cut deeply into her flesh. Her sweat congealed with the grime from the dusty journey, leaving her hide caked with masses of matted fur. Vincente's latest blows to her head drew more blood. It ran down between her eyes, covering her muzzle. The people in the square were horrified and pitied the poor animal. One of the merchants shouted angrily, "Stop before you murder the poor thing!" The group of people encircled Franca and Vincente, with the men now ready to take part in the fight. The rude old man from the leather goods shop used his pent up anger, made a tight fist, and aimed for Vincente's nose, but Vincente was like a wild man and used the rod against him. The man fell to the pavement.

A few of the little children came to the front of the crowd and realized that it was Franca. The same little boy, who had teased Franca the evening before, rushed forward yelling, "No! Not Franca! Let her be!" The little boy threw himself on Franca's neck to protect her. Vincente forcefully shoved the boy aside.

Rascal made his way through the crowd, dodging people's steps and squeezing himself through the tight spaces between people's feet. He was a little dog, but filled with courage. He attacked Vincente by grabbing hold of his ankle. Vincente lowered his stick and swung at the dog, but Rascal was much too quick for him. The dog leaped up and grazed Vincente's hand with his sharp teeth. The brutal weapon dropped. Rascal let himself loose and danced circles around Vincente, yapping furiously. In one great bound, Rascal landed upon the man's back and sunk his teeth into the collar of the cloak. Vincente twirled himself in circles to try to free himself from his new adversary, but Rascal held fast. His little body swung out from the man as he spun in circles.

By now, the crowd in the square had doubled in size. It seemed as if all of the townspeople had collected there. Pietro wiggled his way through the crowd and saw Franca and Rascal there, in the middle of the uproar. He was proud of Rascal for defending her but was sickened at the sight of Franca, battered and sore. He wondered at the pack on her back and guessed at the meaning of the scene.

Once more, Franca's energy was ignited. She kicked Vincente again with her hind legs and hit her mark again. Rascal let go of his grip at the same time, as Vincente was thrown back and collided with the ground. Vincente landed, looking like a crumpled heap on the cobblestone. No more did he come at Franca. Rascal crouched, like a rabid dog, snarling and yelping at Vincente, until Pietro called him off. The magistrate forced himself through the crowd, gathering four men standing nearest to the brutal scene, and swiftly carried Vincente out of the square. Martino fell on his knees, his body and mind tired of the fight. Pietro hastened to his side, to comfort and console him.

Gemma could hear the shouting from where she was working in the inn and had come as fast as she could, troubled by the yelling of the townspeople. She struggled to pass through the multitude but now stood in the center. She saw Franca and, taking her apron, approached to wipe the blood from the poor animal's face.

From the open door of St. Silvestro's church, Don Bartolomeo could see the events unfolding. He had watched as the trio entered through the gates of Turin, taking note of the donkey with the cumbersome load and the two men guiding her. To him, the scene looked odd, so when the shouting started, it did not take him long to become part of the action. He ran first, leaving Alessandro and Giorgio standing in front of the church for a few seconds. Together they turned and rushed after him. By now, they all realized that Franca was in the middle of the commotion.

The crowd opened to let Don Bartolomeo pass with Giorgio right on his heels. "Franca!" Giorgio yelled, "Franca!" When he got close to her, he was shocked at the terrible sight. In that moment, his shouting was outdone by the ringing of the evening *Angelus* bells. Franca, ready to collapse, sensed the time of day and believed Giorgio to be near. She was glad to be back home, and taking her cue from the sound of the bells, she bowed and fell to her knees in the square. Part of her hoped to claim her prize of sugar, part of her wanted just to rest. She was so happy to be near Giorgio again, but she made no sound.

As Franca knelt in the courtyard in front of St. Silvestro's church, the bundle of holy things toppled off her back. The whole pile came loose and scattered on the ground.

Don Bartolomeo stood in the center, with Martino and Pietro on one side, and Franca and the pack on the other. He placed his hands kindly on Martino's shoulder for a brief moment and then turned to face the crowd, raising both hands in the air to calm the people. "My children, my children," he said. "Silence, please."

As the *Angelus* bells came to the end of their song, the gold and silver pieces clattered and

clanged as they spilled out of the pack. Candlesticks bounced up from cobblestone. The altar
bells "chinged" once as they hit the pavement
and then lay silent. The sacred chalice rolled
across the courtyard along with the other things.
Precious items scattered everywhere. The people did not know what to think, but it was what
happened next that changed their hearts forever.

As the monstrance fell upon the cobblestone,
the clasp broke open. The Eucharistic Host
rose into the air by some invisible power. The

townspeople stood in wonderment as the Sacred Host floated freely above their heads. The entire assembly, witnessing the miracle with their own eyes, fell on their knees and worshipped.

The man who sold the leather goods was among the first to fall to his knees. In an instant, his heart turned toward God. He wept and prayed, "Lord, have mercy on me."

"We have a miracle! Praise almighty God! Forgive us, Lord!" others said.

"It is Jesus!" the little boy cried out. "Shining as bright as the sun. The Sun of Justice!"

"Yes," the people in the crowd cheered, "the Sun of Justice!"

The Host stopped rising when it was out of reach, mysteriously suspended above the heads of the people. It hung there in the sky, like a second sun. Some of the people covered their eyes, for the glow of its light created a magnificent aura. Brilliant rays of light shot forth from the Host.

Don Bartolomeo fell prostrate and prayed. The crowded square was filled with people kneeling and praising God. The priest stood, blessed the crowd, and then ran to find the Bishop. He raced all the way, rejoicing that God deemed to give this miraculous gift to his people.

It did not take Don Bartolomeo long to

return with the Bishop. Bishop Ludovico arrived in the square, properly vested and walking in solemn procession with other priests and some noblemen of Turin. Candles were passed around to the people congregating in the square. When the Bishop arrived at the place of the miracle, he fell on his knees and worshiped. He prayed, "Stay with us, Lord."

Don Bartolomeo humbly presented the silver chalice to the Bishop. Bishop Ludovico raised it up high, under the Host. The whole crowd

watched in amazement as the Host easily descended into the chalice without the bishop's aid. With their candles, kindled by the fire of faith renewed, the entire crowd of people followed in procession as the Bishop led them all to the Cathedral of St. John the Baptist. Don Bartolomeo followed the Bishop's lead, walking with one arm stretched around Martino's shoulder. Right behind him walked Pietro, now joined with his father, carrying Rascal in his arms.

As the townspeople walked on, Franca got up from the ground and took some sugar from Giorgio's hand. She was happy to be home again, but she was so tired and sore. Gemma used her apron now and delicately wiped the blood from Franca's face. Alessandro cut away the cords that remained around Franca's middle. Her bleeding wounds oozed with fresh blood.

"Come on, Franca, we've got to get you home. Can you make it to the stable?" Giorgio asked. He was fighting back his tears. He was so happy to have Franca back, but he was feeling so sorry about what she must have endured.

Alessandro stepped in. "Giorgio, I'll carry her if she needs me to," he said.

With Giorgio on one side and Alessandro on the other, Franca began to take the last few steps of her journey. Gemma was with them, too, patting Franca and talking gently to her as they walked along. Giorgio smiled as together they crossed the courtyard. He remembered his prayer for a miracle. Yes, his prayers were answered, he thought to himself. Franca had come home, and his father and all of the people of Turin were renewed in the faith. This was Giorgio's miracle.